The Healing House
Essential Feng Shui

Haruki Nishimura

Booklas Publishing — 2025
Work originally written in 2022

Original Title:
The Healing House – Essential Feng Shui
Copyright © 2025, published by Luiz Antonio dos Santos ME.
This is a non-fiction work exploring practices and concepts in the field of energetic space harmonization. Through an integrative approach, the author offers foundational principles of Feng Shui, biophilic design, and Eastern philosophies to transform physical environments into allies for emotional, spiritual, and physical well-being.

1st Edition
Production Team
Author: Haruki Nishimura
Editor: Luiz Santos
Cover Design: Studios Booklas / Elwyn Darrow
Consultant: Marek Solana
Researchers: Tessa Mirov / Nilo Ardent / Kai Venn
Layout & Typesetting: Corin Elrae

Publishing and Identification
The Healing House – Essential Feng Shui
Booklas, 2025
Categories: Feng Shui / Interior Design / Spirituality
DDC: 133.3337 – **CDU:** 133.5

All rights reserved to:
Luiz Antonio dos Santos ME / Booklas
No part of this book may be reproduced, stored in a retrieval system, or transmitted in any form — electronic, mechanical, photocopying, recording, or otherwise — without the prior and express written permission of the copyright holder.

Summary

Systematic Index 5
Prologue 10
Chapter 1 Space and Life 14
Chapter 2 Feng Shui 23
Chapter 3 Biophilic Design 32
Chapter 4 Vital Energy 41
Chapter 5 Yin and Yang 50
Chapter 6 Five Elements 60
Chapter 7 Tao and Nature 69
Chapter 8 Wabi-Sabi Aesthetics 78
Chapter 9 Zen and Space 87
Chapter 10 Vastu Shastra 95
Chapter 11 Attentive Observation 104
Chapter 12 Senses of Space 112
Chapter 13 Intention and Purpose 120
Chapter 14 Bagua Map 128
Chapter 15 Light and Color 139
Chapter 16 Natural Materials 147
Chapter 17 Living Elements 155
Chapter 18 Sound and Scent 162
Chapter 19 Intentional Art 171
Chapter 20 Free Space 179
Chapter 21 Energetic Cleansing 187
Chapter 22 Harmonious Entrance 195

Chapter 23 Harmonious Living Room 203
Chapter 24 Nourishing Kitchen 212
Chapter 25 Tranquil Bedroom 220
Chapter 26 Invigorating Bathroom 230
Chapter 27 Productive Office 239
Chapter 28 Sacred Space 247
Chapter 29 Living Garden 256
Chapter 30 Health and Vitality 265
Chapter 31 Fluid Creativity 274
Chapter 32 Emotional Balance 281
Chapter 33 Lasting Harmony 288
Epilogue 294

Systematic Index

Chapter 1: Space and Life - Explores the deep connection between the physical home environment and the inhabitant's inner state, psyche, and life experiences.

Chapter 2: Feng Shui - Introduces the ancient Chinese art of Feng Shui, focusing on harmonizing spaces to improve the flow of vital energy (Chi) for well-being.

Chapter 3: Biophilic Design - Discusses the importance of integrating natural elements and patterns into built environments to satisfy the innate human need for connection with nature.

Chapter 4: Vital Energy - Delves into the concept of Chi (Qi), the universal vital energy, and how its flow or stagnation within the home affects residents' well-being.

Chapter 5: Yin and Yang - Explains the fundamental Taoist principles of Yin and Yang and how their dynamic balance shapes the energy and atmosphere of different spaces.

Chapter 6: Five Elements - Details the theory of the Five Elements (Wood, Fire, Earth, Metal, and Water) in Feng Shui and their cycles, used to balance environmental energies.

Chapter 7: Tao and Nature - Explores the Taoist philosophy of living in harmony with the natural flow (Tao) and its application to inhabiting spaces with simplicity and acceptance.

Chapter 8: Wabi-Sabi Aesthetics - Introduces the Japanese aesthetic of Wabi-Sabi, which finds beauty in imperfection, impermanence, and the authenticity of natural materials and aging.

Chapter 9: Zen and Space - Discusses Zen principles applied to space, emphasizing simplicity, minimalism, mindfulness, and creating environments conducive to inner peace.

Chapter 10: Vastu Shastra - Presents the ancient Indian science of Vastu Shastra, focusing on aligning dwellings with cosmic energies through orientation, geometry, and elemental balance.

Chapter 11: Attentive Observation - Emphasizes the crucial first step of truly seeing and feeling the home environment with sensory and intuitive presence before making changes.

Chapter 12: Senses of Space - Highlights the importance of all senses (smell, hearing, touch, taste, sight) in perceiving and shaping the home's atmosphere and overall well-being.

Chapter 13: Intention and Purpose - Focuses on the power of defining a clear intention and purpose for each room to align its energy with the inhabitant's goals and needs.

Chapter 14: Bagua Map - Explains the Feng Shui tool of the Bagua Map, which relates specific areas of the home to corresponding life aspects (career, relationships, etc.).

Chapter 15: Light and Color - Explores the profound impact of natural and artificial light, as well as the vibrational influence of colors, on mood, energy, and spatial harmony.

Chapter 16: Natural Materials - Discusses the benefits of using natural materials (wood, stone, fibers, etc.) for their authentic texture, energetic vitality, and connection to nature.

Chapter 17: Living Elements - Highlights the importance of incorporating living elements like plants, moving water, and pets to bring vitality and natural energy into the home.

Chapter 18: Sound and Scent - Examines the subtle yet powerful influence of the home's soundscape and aromas on mood, energy levels, and the overall atmosphere.

Chapter 19: Intentional Art - Explores using art and decoration not just aesthetically, but as intentional symbols reflecting personal values and desired energies.

Chapter 20: Free Space - Discusses the necessity of creating and maintaining free, uncluttered space for vital energy (Chi) to flow and for releasing stagnant patterns.

Chapter 21: Energetic Cleansing - Details various methods (smudging, sound, salt, light) for purifying the home's subtle energy field, removing negativity and restoring vibrancy.

Chapter 22: Harmonious Entrance - Focuses on the crucial importance of the home's entrance (the "mouth of Chi") and how to create a welcoming, energetically positive threshold.

Chapter 23: Harmonious Living Room - Offers guidance on creating a balanced and welcoming living room, the social heart of the home, fostering connection and relaxation.

Chapter 24: Nourishing Kitchen - Addresses the kitchen as the home's vital center for health and abundance, emphasizing conscious food preparation and organization.

Chapter 25: Tranquil Bedroom - Provides insights into designing the bedroom as a sanctuary for deep rest, regeneration, and intimacy, focusing on calm and security.

Chapter 26: Invigorating Bathroom - Discusses transforming the bathroom into a space for purification and renewal, managing energy flow and promoting self-care rituals.

Chapter 27: Productive Office - Explores creating a home office environment that supports focus, concentration, and the manifestation of professional purpose.

Chapter 28: Sacred Space - Guides the creation of a dedicated personal space within the home for meditation, prayer, introspection, and connection with the sacred.

Chapter 29: Living Garden - Discusses integrating nature through gardens (external or internal), balconies, or potted plants, highlighting the benefits for well-being and connection.

Chapter 30: Health and Vitality - Explores how the home environment directly impacts physical health and vitality through factors like light, air quality, order, and rest.

Chapter 31: Fluid Creativity - Examines how to design a home that stimulates and supports the creative process through space, inspiration, and acceptance of flow.

Chapter 32: Emotional Balance - Discusses how the home environment can act as a sanctuary and support system for achieving and maintaining emotional equilibrium.

Chapter 33: Lasting Harmony - Addresses how to maintain the achieved harmony in the home over time through continuous listening, adaptation, rituals, and gratitude.

Prologue

There are places one merely visits. And there are spaces that inhabit us. This book is a map—not one that leads you to a destination, but one that guides you back home. I'm not talking about the house as a building. I speak of the essential dwelling. Of the inner refuge that pulses beneath every tile, within each wall, under the silent noises of everyday life.

Have you paid attention to your home today? Perhaps you noticed the creaking door, the light that insists on not reaching the darkest corner, or that plant that has been asking for water for days. But have you realized what all this reveals about you?

This book asserts, with courage and clarity: the home is not merely a backdrop where life unfolds—it is life itself made concrete. Everything that vibrates outside echoes within. Everything organized in space also organizes itself in the soul.

Here, you won't find empty promises. You will find revelations. With each chapter, you will be led to decipher silent messages hidden in objects, hallways, and unconscious choices.

The proposal is not to decorate the home, but to awaken it. And, by awakening it, allow yourself to be touched by it. Allow yourself to understand the depth of a poorly positioned mirror, the uncomfortable silence of a lifeless wall, the stagnant energy of a cluttered corner.

Everything speaks. And what this book does, with cutting delicacy, is teach you how to listen.

There is an invisible code that governs spaces. A secret rhythm that connects the sound of leaves to the flow of Chi, that aligns the bed's orientation with the fluidity of emotions, that balances the chaos of a room with the mental field of its inhabitants. Mastering this code is more than aesthetics—it is vital wisdom.

You will be introduced to ancient traditions like Feng Shui, Vastu Shastra, and Zen philosophy, not as Eastern exoticisms, but as ancestral languages of healing.

You will discover that each room is an archetypal mirror of the psyche: the kitchen nourishes, the bathroom purifies, the bedroom regenerates, the entrance welcomes or repels. Each space contains a primary energy, and understanding this is the beginning of healing, not just the house—but the story that unfolds within it.

This book doesn't teach you how to reside. It teaches you how to inhabit. To inhabit with presence, with reverence, with deep listening.

Every word here carries an invitation to return to the essential. To reclaim the sacredness that exists in the gesture of opening a window, lighting a candle, removing the excess. Yes, there is beauty in emptiness. There is order in simplicity. And there is power in intention.

The wisdom contained herein is not limited to one culture or time. It resonates at the core of what it means to live meaningfully. It is applied philosophy. Psychology of space. Medicine of the home. Therapy of form.

It is knowledge that transforms every environment into a healing mirror, and every movement within it into a ritual of alignment.

You will feel the call to reorganize the house not as a domestic chore, but as a ritual act. Decluttering will no longer be about physical space, but about releasing traumas and invisible burdens. The light entering the bedroom will cease to be a physical phenomenon and will become a symbol of the consciousness wishing to illuminate its shadow.

This is the real impact of the work you hold in your hands.

But be warned: this is not a book to be read passively. It is a mirror-book. A door-book. A book that asks for courage. Courage to see what has been ignored, to listen to what has been silenced, to harmonize what was in conflict.

Because by harmonizing the house, one harmonizes the soul. By purifying the environment, one purifies destiny.

With each page, you will notice something awakening. A subtle urgency. A sweet restlessness. A call for lightness, for truth, for belonging.

By the end, you will not be the same—because the house you inhabit will no longer be the same either.

Therefore, reader, prepare yourself. Take a deep breath before starting this reading. Not because it is difficult, but because it is true. And all truth, when it arrives, demands space.

Open yourself. Observe. Feel. And allow yourself to be healed.

You are about to enter *The Healing House*—and in doing so, perhaps discover that the one most in need of healing wasn't the house. It was you.

Luiz Santos Editor

Chapter 1
Space and Life

The home we inhabit is far more than just a collection of walls, doors, and windows, a mere physical stage where the pre-established routines of our days unfold. It breathes, pulses, reacts like a living organism, attuned to the subtle rhythms, the contained joys, and the emotional storms of those who dwell within it. There exists a deep connection, almost ethereal yet undeniably concrete, intertwining the environment that surrounds us with our most intimate inner state. This isn't a one-way street; it's a constant dialogue, a silent exchange of energies and influences.

Each room functions as a tangible extension of our psyche, a three-dimensional mirror reflecting not only aesthetic tastes but also deep layers of our personality, our hidden fears, our dearest dreams. Every object placed there, from the carefully chosen piece of art to the most mundane utensil, reveals untold stories, choices made consciously or unconsciously, guarded silences, memories that insist on lingering. The way everything is organized, or disorganized, in the physical space is a precise map of who we are, a biography written without words, readable to anyone willing to observe attentively. Our external space, from this perspective, is a continuous and relentless revelation of our internal space.

That forgotten pile of papers on the desk, growing day by day under the pretext of lacking time, might symbolize much more than superficial disorganization. It could be the reflection of postponed decisions, projects shelved for fear of failure or success, difficult conversations we avoid having, clarity we fear finding. The sunken sofa, with its frayed fabric and tired springs, isn't just a testament to the natural wear imposed by time; it might mirror our own neglect of true rest, a symbol of the difficulty in allowing ourselves full comfort, guilt-free relaxation. The bare walls, colorless, lacking pictures that tell stories, without the vibration of a soul expressing itself, perhaps speak louder than we'd like about an absence of personal expression, about a life lived in neutral tones, suspended in an indefinite wait for something to awaken it.

The physical environment around us isn't a passive backdrop; it acts as an active participant in our life experience. Environmental psychologists have studied for decades how architecture, interior design, the presence or absence of nature, and spatial organization affect our mood, cognition, behavior, and overall well-being. A chaotic space, for example, with excessive visual stimuli and disorder, is proven to increase levels of cortisol, the stress hormone, making concentration difficult and promoting feelings of anxiety and overload. The human mind seeks patterns and order to feel secure; external disorder generates constant internal noise, a background tension that undermines vital energy.

Similarly, dark, poorly lit environments or those without access to natural light can contribute to feelings of discouragement, lethargy, and even depression, as sunlight is crucial for regulating our biological clock and producing well-being-associated neurotransmitters like serotonin. A home that breathes, welcomes light, allows air circulation, and flows without visual or physical obstacles almost invariably reveals a more awake soul, more conscious of itself and its surroundings. When we pay attention to details, when every corner of the house, however simple, holds a clear intention – be it for rest, work, socializing, or contemplation – life begins to unfold with more meaning, more purpose. We notice an unexpected lightness in our days, greater clarity in the decisions we need to make, a more intense presence in the moments that make up our existence.

This isn't about empty mysticism or magical thinking; it's an empirical observation that spans cultures and times. Ancient wisdom, like Feng Shui itself which we will explore further, already pointed to this intrinsic connection between humans and their habitat, reaching even contemporary environmental psychology, which validates with scientific data the profound influence of the environment on our physical and mental health. Everything around us, every object, color, texture, sound, or silence, influences us continuously and cumulatively. And, reciprocally, everything we touch, organize, choose to compose our space carries back our energy, our intention, our history. There is a constant exchange, a vibrational field formed in this interaction.

For this fundamental reason, understanding the environment not as an inert collection of matter, but as a living, pulsating language, is the essential first step for anyone wishing to redesign their own life, starting from the inside out. The transformation of the external space acts as a powerful catalyst for internal transformation. Moving a piece of furniture can symbolically unlock a rigid mental perspective. Deep cleaning a forgotten closet can clear the way for new thoughts, new possibilities that previously seemed blocked.

The Eastern philosophy of Feng Shui, an ancient Chinese art dedicated to harmonizing spaces to promote the flow of vital energy (Chi), points with remarkable precision to this intrinsic connection between environment and well-being. Its principles teach that every element present in our home, every choice of spatial arrangement, every shade of color selected for a wall, every shape of a decorative object – none of this is the result of chance or mere aesthetic preference. There is a direct correspondence, an energetic mirroring, between how we organize our physical environment and the various aspects of our existence – emotional, mental, relational, and even spiritual.

Living immersed in a chaotic, dark, stuffy space, where the air feels heavy and energy stagnates, is not just a physical or visual discomfort; it functions as a real impediment to the healthy flow of vital energy. It's a silent, often unconscious limitation that contaminates mood, mental clarity, productivity, and ultimately, even physical health. External disorder generates internal noise that hinders peace and concentration.

Inhabiting an environment that breathes light, allows the natural circulation of energies, where beauty manifests in simplicity and intention, where harmony and functionality walk together, is not just aesthetically pleasing – it represents a deep and powerful form of self-care. It's like giving explicit permission to the soul to expand, to breathe freely, to find its space for expression in the world.

When we begin to look at our home with these more attentive, sensitive eyes, we discover that it observes us back. It tells us stories about ourselves that perhaps we preferred to ignore. That forgotten corner in the back of the room, where unused objects, boxes closed for years, unopened gifts always accumulate, might be revealing a part of our own life that is also abandoned, neglected, waiting for attention and care. An area of our psyche we fear exploring. A bathroom one never enters with pleasure, that always seems cold, impersonal, or disorganized, might symbolize a difficult relationship with one's own body, with self-acceptance, or with the necessary rituals of purification and renewal. The way we treat the space dedicated to cleansing the physical body often mirrors how we deal with our emotional and mental cleansing. The poorly lit bedroom, where sleep is restless and awakening tired, might reflect an internal resistance to true rest, to letting go of tensions accumulated during the day, a difficulty in surrendering to the natural cycle of nightly regeneration.

And when this symbolic reading of space becomes conscious, when we perceive the messages the house sends us silently, a new cycle of transformation can finally begin. The power lies in bringing to light what was hidden in the shadow of habit.

The force of transformation doesn't necessarily reside in major renovations or hefty investments. It almost always begins with small gestures imbued with intention. Moving a piece of furniture, breaking an old pattern of circulation, can unlock a mental or emotional stagnation that seemed insurmountable. Performing a deep cleaning, not just superficially, but opening closets, drawers, emptying boxes, can clear the way for new thoughts, new ideas, a renewed sense of clarity. Changing the bed's position to one offering more security and welcome, placing a living, thriving plant in the living room to bring nature's energy inside, allowing sunlight to flood a room that previously lived in gloom – these are seemingly simple actions, yet they carry immense potential to redefine entire internal narratives.

The house, then, ceases to be a fixed, immutable setting and becomes a dynamic ally, a living, pulsating extension of our personal journey of growth and self-knowledge. The home acts as an unforgiving mirror. It reflects not only our preferred aesthetic, but what we tolerate in ourselves and others, what we deeply value, what we feed with our attention and energy, and what we, consciously or unconsciously, allow to die from lack of care. It is also our starting point and our safe harbor. Everything we experience out there, on the world stage, begins to gestate here within, in the intimacy of our refuge. The most important decisions are rarely made in the turmoil of the street or the bustle of the office; they are born in the reflective calm of the kitchen while preparing tea, in the introspective silence of the bathroom during a long bath, in the welcoming intimacy of the bedroom before falling asleep. The world outside is, to a large extent, a consequence of the world we cultivate inside. And this inner world begins to take shape, to gain substance, in the physical space we call home.

There is, resonating in this theme, a deep ancestral question, a wisdom that vibrates through the ages. Ancient peoples, across various cultures, knew instinctively that the dwelling was a sacred space, a microcosm reflecting the macrocosm. A house wasn't built randomly, without considering the forces of nature. The entrance wasn't positioned arbitrarily, ignoring energy flows. One didn't sleep in just any corner, misaligned with cosmic rhythms. The house was oriented by the stars, the sun's path, the vital presence of water, the prevailing direction of the winds. It was conceived and inhabited as a temple. Today, by reclaiming this lost sensitivity, by looking again at our dwelling with reverence, we give it not only functional comfort but existential dignity. We treat it again with the respect it deserves, and it, in return, gives us back this energy in the form of vitality, well-being, clarity, and protection.

When we use the expression "redesigning space and life," we aren't just speaking of a poetic metaphor; we are describing a functional truth, a real psychophysical dynamic. Repositioning objects to create a more harmonious flow, cleaning what is dirty and stagnant, illuminating what lives in darkness, opening what has been locked away for a long time – all these concrete actions in the physical environment act as a powerful invitation for the same transformations to occur within the soul. It's a direct mirroring. Some complain about being unable to break a negative cycle, feeling stuck in life, yet fail to realize they live immersed in a disordered room, perhaps foul-smelling, stifled by lack of air and light. How can the mind expand, generate new ideas, find creative solutions, if the physical body inhabits a place that energetically represses it? The connection is direct.

By caring for the house with attention and intention, one cares for the energy that envelops and fills it. And this renewed, balanced energy begins to nourish those who live there. There's no need for large, expensive renovations or hiring costly experts to begin this process. True transformation begins with awareness. It starts with the simple act of opening a window and truly noticing how much light actually enters that room. It begins with the attitude of sitting on the floor, in silence, and observing what the house communicates through its shapes, colors, sounds, smells, voids. And when this attentive listening settles in, when the silent dialogue between inhabitant and habitat is re-established, the magic begins to happen.

The beauty of an approach like existential Feng Shui lies precisely in this point: it unites profound philosophy and everyday practice. It doesn't impose rigid formulas or universal rules, but invites attentive observation, sensitivity, intuition. It doesn't speak of fleeting decorative fads, but of energetic coherence, of alignment between space and being. It shows us that it's perfectly possible to create environments where the body finds restorative rest, the mind finds clarity, and the spirit feels truly at home, belonging, secure. And, by doing so, by redesigning the space with this awareness, one inevitably designs a new biography, a new way of walking through life.

The house you live in today might be physically the same as yesterday, but it will never be the same again after being touched by a conscious gaze, by an intentional act of care. And the same principle applies to your life. The same story can gain new colors, new flows, new meanings – just by changing how you walk through it, the perspective with which you look at events. A reorganized environment, harmonized with nature's principles, purified of excesses and stagnant energies, becomes fertile ground for deep and lasting internal changes.

Because, deep down, we understand that home is not just the physical space where we live. It is the symbolic territory where our life is written, day after day. And every space, like every story, can be rewritten – with clear intention, deep respect, and attentive listening. The house is where being finds concrete form, where the invisible becomes visible, where our inner world gains ground, structure, manifestation. Caring for the house, in this broad and deep sense, is a revolutionary act of self-care, because it is, ultimately, caring for one's own destiny, one's own evolutionary journey.

Chapter 2
Feng Shui

In the deepest, most ancient roots of the vast Chinese civilization, a silent wisdom flourished, an intuitive understanding of the world passed down through generations not primarily through written texts or rigid dogmas, but through the delicate, patient, and reverent observation of nature and the subtle, yet powerful way it influenced absolutely everything around – the weather, harvests, animal health, and crucially, the well-being and fortune of human beings. From this attentive observation, this deep attunement to terrestrial and celestial rhythms, Feng Shui was born, an art and science that far transcends simple interior decoration or the mere strategic placement of objects within a space.

Feng Shui is, first and foremost, a comprehensive way of understanding the world as a living, interconnected system, and the specific place that we, as individuals and as a community, occupy within this complex and dynamic existential fabric. The very name of this millennial practice reveals much about its philosophical essence: "Feng" means Wind, the invisible force, the vital breath that carries seeds, shapes dunes, moves clouds, and disperses energies; "Shui" means Water, the fluid, adaptable element, essential to life, which bypasses obstacles, nourishes the earth, reflects the sky, and accumulates energy in its stillness. Wind and Water are thus two of the most subtle and penetrating forces of nature, yet simultaneously capable of shaping mountains over millennia and carving deep valleys with their persistence. In Feng Shui thinking, they are seen as the primordial conductors of universal vital energy, the force that animates all things, known as Chi (or Qi). They are the invisible messengers that distribute this energy throughout the environment, influencing the quality of life in a given location.

With a history dating back over four thousand years, possibly intertwined with shamanic practices and astronomical observation of the early Chinese dynasties, Feng Shui originated from the empirical observation that the arrangement of elements in a space – whether natural, like mountains, rivers, and trees, or built, like buildings, walls, and furniture – directly influences the flow of Chi in that location. And consequently, this quality of energy flow profoundly affects the physical and mental health, material prosperity, emotional balance, relationship harmony, and even the spiritual dimension of the individuals who live or work there. It's not a superstitious belief, but a complex system that seeks to understand and apply the natural laws governing the flow of energy in the built environment, in resonance with the surrounding natural environment.

At the pulsating heart of Feng Shui lies the fundamental principle of harmony with nature. In a modern world where humans often try to impose their dominion over the environment, controlling, modifying, and often destroying ecosystems in the name of progress or immediate comfort, Feng Shui teaches the exact opposite path: living in tune, in respectful dialogue, in intelligent cooperation with natural forces. This involves carefully observing seasonal cycles, subtle energy flows, the presence and movement of sunlight throughout the day, the preferred natural paths of the wind, the way water moves and accumulates in the landscape. And, based on this deep observation, creating spaces – homes, offices, gardens, cities – that do not oppose this vital flow, but welcome it, gently direct it, and enhance it for the benefit of all. It's a philosophy of integration, not domination.

The practical application of this ancient wisdom invariably begins with looking. But not a superficial look, trained only to perceive aesthetic forms and colors. It's a gaze that seeks to perceive what is invisible to ordinary eyes, that feels the energy of the place, the atmosphere hovering in each room. When an environment feels uncomfortable for no apparent reason, when we feel inexplicable fatigue while staying in certain rooms of the house, when things in life seem stagnant, blocked, lacking fluidity, Feng Shui indicates that the Chi in that space is likely obstructed, blocked, or unbalanced. This obstruction can be caused by seemingly insignificant factors: poorly positioned furniture interrupting circulation, an excessive accumulation of purposeless objects suffocating the environment, a wall color energetically unbalancing the space for its function, a door that doesn't open completely, symbolizing lost or limited opportunities.

Small details that, gathered and accumulated over time, create major consequences in the energetic field and, by extension, in the inhabitants' lives.

This sensitivity to the energy of space is not merely subjective or esoteric; it manifests in concrete, observable results in people's lives. There are countless reports of individuals who, after consciously applying Feng Shui principles in their homes or workplaces, observed significant improvements in various aspects such as increased concentration and focus, stimulation of creativity, improved sleep quality and reduced insomnia, greater mental clarity for making important decisions, and even relief from physical and emotional health issues. This happens because, according to Feng Shui theory, by removing blockages and harmonizing the environment, the vital energy (Chi) flows again with more freedom and vitality. And where energy circulates healthily and balanced, life flourishes in all its dimensions. The environment ceases to be a passive obstacle and becomes an active support for well-being and personal development.

Among the various tools Feng Shui uses to diagnose and harmonize spaces, furniture placement is one of the best known and most impactful. A bed directly facing the bedroom door, for example, is considered a vulnerable position, as the person lying down has no visual control over who enters, which can generate an unconscious feeling of insecurity, restlessness, and difficulty relaxing deeply. A desk facing a solid wall can symbolically block the flow of ideas, future vision, and creative inspiration. A large sofa positioned to impede free circulation in the living room not only hinders physical movement but can also interrupt the flow of conversation, social interaction, and the energy itself in the environment. Reorganizing the space according to Feng Shui principles, like the "command position" (where one has a view of the door but isn't directly aligned with it), is not about following arbitrary aesthetic rules, but about allowing the environment to breathe energetically, offering psychological security, and facilitating the natural flows of life.

Colors also play a fundamental role in Feng Shui practice. Each tone, each hue, carries a specific energetic vibration, and its presence in an environment directly affects the emotional, mental, and energetic field of those within it. Vibrant red, for example, activates the Fire element's energy, stimulating passion, action, celebration, and recognition; it should be used cautiously, as excess can generate agitation or conflict. Deep blue brings the calm and introspection of the Water element, promoting serenity, reflection, and communication flow; ideal for bedrooms or meditation spaces, but excess can lead to melancholy. Green evokes the vitality and growth of the Wood element, with its energy of renewal, health, and expansion; great for living rooms, kitchens, or study areas. The conscious choice of colors in an environment goes far beyond mere personal taste or decoration trends; it is intrinsically linked to the energetic intention one wishes to nurture and cultivate in each specific space of the house, aligning it with its primary function.

Another powerful symbolic resource used by Feng Shui is the strategic use of representative elements, which act as anchors for specific energies in the environment. A small indoor water fountain, with clean, flowing water, is not just a pleasant decorative object; it symbolizes the flow of abundance, prosperity, and fluidity in life, activating wealth energy when correctly positioned (usually in the Prosperity Gua). A multi-faceted crystal hanging in the window not only reflects sunlight into rainbows across the room; it activates Chi movement, disperses stagnant energies, and purifies the subtle atmosphere of the place. A well-placed mirror serves not only to reflect physical images; it can also be used to visually expand space, symbolically duplicate positive intentions (like reflecting a bountiful dining table or a beautiful view), correct missing areas in the floor plan, or beneficially redirect energy flow. Every object can be imbued with meaning and intention.

At the center of this millennial practice lies the profound concept that every environment, every house, possesses its own soul, a kind of individual energy field that can be strengthened through care and intention, or weakened by neglect and disharmony. When the space is treated with respect, attention to detail, and awareness of its influence, it reciprocates with welcome, protection, and energetic support. Therefore, Feng Shui should not be reduced to a set of ready-made formulas to be applied mechanically, or to fleeting decorative fads that quickly lose meaning. It requires sensitive listening, attentive presence, and the development of an intimate, personal relationship with the space one inhabits. One must feel the place, dialogue with it, perceive its energetic needs.

The philosophy behind Feng Shui is also deeply spiritual, though not necessarily religious. It is intrinsically linked to the idea that everything in the universe is energy in different states of vibration – people, animals, plants, objects, shapes, colors, sounds, scents. Nothing is neutral. Everything constantly emits and receives energy. Everything vibrates in resonance or dissonance with what surrounds it. And by organizing our physical environment, we are not just moving chairs, painting walls, or hanging pictures; we are, in fact, reprogramming the subtle field of our own existence, realigning the energies that surround us, and consequently, influencing our life trajectory. The space becomes both a reflection and a catalyst for our inner journey.

It is crucial to understand that Feng Shui does not impose rules authoritatively. It proposes paths. It observes the energetic dynamics of a space, analyzes flows, identifies imbalances, and suggests interventions so that the environment becomes a powerful ally, not a silent obstacle, on the path to a fuller, healthier, and more prosperous life. And it does so based on principles that respect both the logic of observing nature and the practitioner's intuition. It's not about strictly following a rigid manual, but about learning the subtle language of the house, listening to what it tells us through its signs, and responding to it with wisdom, intention, and respect.

Some of the fundamental concepts underpinning this millennial practice, such as the dynamic balance between the complementary forces Yin and Yang, the theory of the Five Elements (Wood, Fire, Earth, Metal, and Water) and their cycles of generation and control, and the application of the Bagua Map with its nine Guas corresponding to essential life areas, will be explored in the following chapters, offering more specific tools for harmonization. But before diving into these techniques, what needs to blossom internally is a sincere disposition, a genuine desire to live in harmony with space, to recognize its influence, and to co-create with it an atmosphere of well-being.

Because Feng Shui, despite its antiquity, remains profoundly current – perhaps even more necessary than ever in a contemporary world where we live increasingly disconnected from nature, immersed in artificial, closed, electronic, and energetically impoverished environments. Rediscovering this ancestral art is, in essence, reconnecting with the natural rhythm of things, with the intrinsic wisdom of the universe reflected in our own home.

The house, seen through the lens of Feng Shui, ceases to be a passive, neutral container and reveals itself as a dynamic force field, a living organism that interacts with us. Each object, wall, cardinal direction becomes a pulsating energy point, a subtle vortex influencing our state of being. And the resident ceases to be just a passive occupant to become a co-creator of atmospheres, a conscious healer of space, a true gardener of the energy circulating there. This is the essential invitation of Feng Shui: to live with expanded awareness, move through space with clear intention, inhabit the home with reverence and gratitude. Because the place where we live is also the place where our soul rests, regenerates, and dreams. And when the home vibrates in harmony with the subtle laws of nature, everything around seems to respond with more beauty, fluidity, abundance, and peace. The transformation of space inevitably reflects in the transformation of life.

Chapter 3
Biophilic Design

There is an ancestral memory deeply etched into our skin, in our eyes that seek the green horizon, in our lungs that yearn for pure air, and in the primordial rhythm of our heart. It is nature's insistent call, the indelible memory that we are, before any cultural label or social definition, creatures intrinsically shaped by millennia of intimate coexistence with trees that offered shade and shelter, stones that taught us about solidity and time, rivers that quenched our thirst and guided our paths, vast skies that inspired awe, and fertile earth that nourished us. When we drastically distance ourselves from this original matrix, when we isolate ourselves in boxes of concrete and glass, disconnected from natural cycles, something essential within us begins to ail – often silently, manifesting as chronic stress, diffuse anxiety, lack of vitality, or a persistent sense of existential emptiness.

Biophilic design emerges, in this modern context of increasing urbanization and digitalization, as a conscious and necessary response to this profound disconnection: it is an approach to architecture and interior design that remembers where we came from, recognizes our innate need for connection with the natural world, and seeks to reintegrate nature's elements and patterns into the built environments where we spend most of our lives.

Contrary to what many might imagine, reconnecting with nature through biophilic design doesn't require a radical renunciation of contemporary urban life, nor the abandonment of technologies that facilitate and enrich our modern daily lives. Biophilic design doesn't propose an opposition between the built and the natural, but rather a harmonious integration, an intelligent symbiosis. It doesn't suggest everyone should escape to the forest or live in isolated cabins, but rather that we can bring the essence of the forest, its patterns, textures, vitality, into our homes, offices, schools, and hospitals – even in carefully selected fragments: the vibrant presence of a green leaf, the comforting solidity of a smooth stone, the dance of a sunbeam crossing the window, the relaxing sound of moving water, the organic texture of raw wood. It's about weaving nature back into the fabric of our daily lives.

This concept, though seemingly intuitive, acts as a robust bridge between ancestral wisdom, which always valued harmony with the environment, and the discoveries of contemporary well-being sciences, such as environmental psychology, neuroarchitecture, and integrative medicine. The term "biophilia," literally meaning "love of life" or "innate affinity with living systems," was popularized by the renowned American biologist Edward O. Wilson in the 1980s. Wilson posited that there is an intrinsic, genetically determined tendency in humans to seek connection with nature and other living organisms. This affinity wouldn't just be an aesthetic preference, but a fundamental biological need for our physical and mental health, an evolutionary legacy of our long history as a species immersed in the natural world.

Since then, a growing body of scientific research conducted by architects, designers, doctors, psychologists, and neuroscientists has been proving, with concrete and measurable data, the multiple benefits of this deliberate reconnection with nature in built environments. Studies consistently demonstrate: significant reduction in stress and anxiety levels, increased creativity and problem-solving ability, improved mood and overall sense of well-being, reinforcement of the immune system, acceleration of physical healing processes in hospital settings, and even increased productivity and satisfaction in work environments. Nature, it seems, is a powerful and underutilized remedy.

In our homes, biophilic design manifests through conscious choices that favor direct or indirect contact with natural elements and patterns. Sunlight, for example, is one of the essential protagonists of this approach. Instead of settling for cold, static, and often harsh artificial lighting, the biophilic proposal is to maximize the entry of daylight in all its dynamic variations – the soft, welcoming gold of the morning, the vibrant, energizing white of midday, the peaceful, relaxing orange of the late afternoon. Large windows, skylights, glass doors, mirrors strategically placed to reflect light into darker corners are tools to bring the solar cycle indoors. These natural cycles of light and shadow are crucial for synchronizing our internal biological clock (circadian rhythm), regulating hormone production (like melatonin for sleep and cortisol for stress), directly affecting our mood, and inducing more balanced and resilient mental states. Living in sync with sunlight is living in sync with our own body.

The air we breathe is also treated as a sacred element in biophilic design. Poorly ventilated, closed, and stagnant environments accumulate not only dust and chemical pollutants (often released by building materials and synthetic furniture), but also stagnant energy, the Sha Chi of Feng Shui. Biophilic design favors and promotes natural cross-ventilation, allows the entry of fresh breezes, values easily openable windows, balconies that function as green lungs for the house, and ventilation systems that prioritize constant air renewal. When air flows freely, ideas also flow with more clarity. When oxygen is renewed, the mind becomes more alert, the body more willing, the sense of vitality increases. Breathing pure air indoors should be the norm, not the exception.

Another essential and perhaps the most visible element of biophilic design is the abundant presence of plants. And here it's not just about using green as a final decorative touch; plants are complex living organisms that interact with us and the environment in real-time, in subtle and profound ways. They purify the air by absorbing carbon dioxide and releasing oxygen, as well as filtering harmful volatile organic compounds (VOCs). They help stabilize relative air humidity, making the environment more comfortable. Their leaves can dampen unwanted noise, creating more pleasant acoustics. And, perhaps most importantly, they visually teach us about rhythm, patience, resilience, and regeneration. Watching a plant grow, sprout, bloom, and adapt to environmental conditions is a silent lesson about life cycles. A pot with a lush fern radiates more vitality and well-being than any expensive painting or inert design object. A small herb garden grown in the kitchen window transforms the act of cooking and eating into daily rituals of connection with authentic flavor, the cycle of seasons, the earth, and one's own body.

Natural materials also take absolute center stage in biophilic design. Instead of plasticized furniture, vinyl flooring, laminated surfaces, and synthetic finishes that often emit toxic substances and create a sensory barrier between us and the environment, this approach values the authentic beauty and tactile richness of raw wood or wood with natural finishes, breathable linen, woven straw, organic cotton, porous handmade ceramics, stone with its unique veins. These are textures that invite touch, carry intrinsic warmth, awaken our dormant senses. These materials breathe with the environment, respond to variations in temperature and humidity. They age with dignity, change color with light exposure, accumulate marks of use, and tell stories – and for this very reason, they remind us of life itself, which is also imperfect, impermanent, organic, alive. Touching a solid wood surface is feeling the tree's history; wearing linen clothing is feeling the lightness of the plant fiber.

The sounds of the environment are equally considered with seriousness. The melodious song of birds in the morning, the gentle murmur of running water in a fountain, the rustling of wind among the leaves of a nearby tree – all these natural sounds act as balms for the nervous system, reducing the activity of the sympathetic system (fight or flight) and activating the parasympathetic system (rest and digest). Even in noisy urban environments, it's possible to create this restorative sound atmosphere with the use of indoor or outdoor water features, harmonically tuned wind chimes, aquariums with the gentle bubbling of the filter, or even through the playback of natural soundtracks (like forest, rain, or ocean wave sounds) at a subtle volume. These are auditory stimuli that calm without distracting, filling the space with a positive vibration without saturating it with unnecessary information. Silence is also a valued sound, the absence of noise that allows introspection.

Biophilic design, therefore, cannot be reduced to a mere decorative style with an organic aesthetic. It is a profound philosophy of dwelling, a way of rethinking our relationship with the spaces we create and occupy. It is not limited to adding plants or using wood, but proposes a way of thinking about buildings and interiors as living, interdependent ecosystems that must function in harmony with human biological rhythms and larger natural systems. A clear example of this is the idea of "restorative views": the importance of being able to look out from inside the house and contemplate something green, something moving with the wind, something reminiscent of life pulsating outside. Even if it's just a single plant on the balcony, a distant tree seen from the office window, or a small indoor garden visible from the living room, this view has proven therapeutic power. Studies show that looking at nature, even for just a few minutes, can significantly lower blood pressure, slow breathing, reduce muscle tension, and improve mood almost instantly. Our eyes evolved to seek and appreciate the fractal complexity and vitality of the natural world.

There is also a powerful symbolic dimension to the natural elements brought indoors. Stones rolled from a river, shells found on the beach during vacation, interestingly shaped dry branches, or a small container with sand from a special place are not just inert decorative objects; they are sensory and emotional anchors that reconnect us with experienced landscapes, affective memories, dreams of future travels. A small collection of stones brought back from a family hike carries the energy of that moment, the feeling of belonging, the shared story. A hand-modeled clay pot by a local artisan evokes ancestry, connection to manual labor, the primordial idea that everything comes from the earth and returns to it. These objects tell stories and bring meaning to the space.

In daily practice, you don't need to transform the entire house at once to start enjoying the benefits of biophilic design. A small "nature altar" can be the ideal starting point: a dedicated space where elements representing nature for you are gathered – perhaps a candle for the fire element, a fresh flower or plant for life, a crystal or stone for the earth, a small shell for water, a piece of wood for growth, an image reminiscent of a natural landscape that brings you peace. Small conscious gestures that re-establish the lost dialogue with the Earth, reminding us of our intrinsic connection with the living world.

This deliberate reunion with nature indoors also gradually generates a deeper transformation in our perception: it changes how we see and feel time. Biophilic design, by its very essence, slows down our frantic internal rhythm. It invites contemplation, patient observation of a leaf's growth cycle, subtle perception of changing light throughout the day, respect for the intrinsic rhythm of living things. And by doing so, by attuning us to nature's time, biophilic design invites the inhabitant to rediscover and honor their own internal time – a more organic time, less pressured by external urgency, more authentic and aligned with their real needs for rest, activity, and reflection.

By bringing life – plants, natural light, fresh air, organic materials – into the home, biophilic design also stimulates, almost as a natural consequence, an ethic of responsibility and care. When one coexists daily with plants needing water and light, with living materials that age and react to the environment, with circulating air and entering and exiting light, the desire to preserve, care for, maintain this delicate balance arises spontaneously. The house ceases to be seen merely as a place of passive consumption and begins to be perceived as a space of active care, a small ecosystem dependent on our attention. And this care, this ecological awareness cultivated in the microcosm of the home, tends to extend outward: to the neighborhood, the city, the planet. Living in close contact with nature, even domesticated nature, empirically teaches about interdependence, life and death cycles, limits, and the generosity of abundance when there is balance. It fundamentally teaches that everything is connected.

And so, through the conscious application of biophilic principles, the house transcends its function as mere physical shelter. It transforms into an inhabited garden, a daily sanctuary where body, mind, and spirit find nourishment, calm, and inspiration. Every gesture within this space ceases to be automatic and mechanical, gaining new meaning, new depth. Sunbathing on the balcony becomes a conscious ritual of healing and vitality. Watering the plants in the morning becomes a silent conversation with time and life. Opening the window upon waking is a small offering of gratitude to the light and air that sustain us.

Biophilic design doesn't promise a perfect, aseptic, or immutable house. It promises, instead, a living house – and, like everything alive, it will be imperfect, changeable, full of soul and stories to tell. And a life that unfolds in tune with this environment enriched by nature inevitably becomes fuller, more sensitive, more rooted, and more resilient. Because by cultivating a piece of nature inside the house, it is our own inner nature that we allow to be reborn and flourish.

Chapter 4
Vital Energy

Life, in its deepest and most mysterious essence, manifests through an invisible yet extraordinarily powerful force that permeates, animates, and connects all things in the universe. This subtle force, flowing like a cosmic river through landscapes, living beings, and even inanimate objects, is called Chi in the Feng Shui tradition – or Qi (pronounced "chee"), according to the more common transliteration in traditional Chinese medicine and other Eastern practices.

Chi is not something one can see with physical eyes, measure with conventional scientific instruments, or touch with hands, but it is an energetic reality that can be felt with the body, perceived with an open heart, and intuited with a quieted mind. It is the silent breath that animates the manifest world, the primordial vibration that infiltrates every space, sustains every breath, pulses in every moment of existence. Where Chi circulates freely, harmoniously, and balanced, health, joy, creativity, prosperity, and vitality flourish. Where, conversely, it accumulates excessively, stagnates like still water, or dissipates rapidly, chronic fatigue, physical and emotional discomfort, mental confusion, and imbalance in various areas of life arise.

Understanding and cultivating Chi is, therefore, fundamental for a full life.

The house, as a direct and sensitive extension of the life that inhabits it, as a three-dimensional mirror of our own energy and consciousness, is also traversed and filled by this dynamic energy field. Each room, each object within it, each forgotten or valued corner possesses its own particular flow of Chi – a flow that can be harmonious, nourishing, and revitalizing, or, conversely, turbulent, blocked, and draining.

When we enter an environment and feel an inexplicable unease, a sense of heaviness in the air, a subtle oppression that invites us to leave quickly; when we find ourselves becoming irritated for no apparent reason, anxious, or suddenly drained of energy while staying in certain parts of the house, often the underlying cause, according to the Feng Shui perspective, is that the Chi there is interrupted, trapped, stagnant, or contaminated by remnants of dense emotional energies (like arguments, sadness, or fears) or by the excess of material accumulation and disorder. Vital energy is subtle, almost imperceptible to most people in daily life, but its presence – or its absence and quality – completely shapes our subjective experience of living in that space.

Feng Shui understands that Chi, to promote health and well-being, must flow gently through environments, like a tranquil river meandering through the landscape, nourishing the banks it passes. This ideal flow should be neither too fast, like a rushing current that drags everything with it and generates instability and agitation (known as cutting Sha Chi), nor so slow that it becomes a stagnant swamp, where energy sits still, putrefied, generating lethargy and lack of vitality. The ideal is a flow that nourishes without suffocating, envelops without imprisoning, inspires without dispersing.

For this to happen, the house needs to be organized in a way that allows and encourages this continuous and gentle movement of energy. Entrances (doors and windows) should be unobstructed and functioning well, passages (corridors, spaces between furniture) should be free and inviting, the objects present should bring lightness, beauty, or meaning, and natural elements (light, air, plants, water) should be invited to participate in the home's energy dynamics, inviting presence and well-being.

Environments that are very dark, chronically stuffy due to lack of ventilation, or excessively overloaded with furniture, decorative objects, and accumulated clutter are especially prone to creating zones of Chi stagnation. A room with numerous boxes and objects stored under the bed, cluttered closets with clothes and items unused for years, narrow corridors obstructed by furniture or decorations hindering passage, shelves filled with forgotten, dusty, or broken items – all these are clear signs of stagnant energy, of Chi unable to breathe, circulate, renew itself. This energetic stagnation is not just an aesthetic or organizational issue; it directly interferes with our physiology and psychology. The energetic weight of the environment often translates into persistent mental fatigue, difficulty concentrating, lack of focus, insomnia or non-restorative sleep, unexplained physical aches (especially in the back and shoulders, where tension accumulates), and a general feeling of being "stuck" in life. The external environment reflects and reinforces the internal state.

In stark contrast, an environment that is airy, generously receives natural light, where physical circulation is easy and intuitive, and which contains living elements like plants or moving water, immediately conveys a sense of relief, lightness, and well-being to those who enter. The body relaxes almost instantly, breathing deepens, the mind quiets, the senses open to perceive the beauty of the present moment. This pleasant sensation reflects Chi flowing freely, like a fresh, revitalizing breeze on a hot summer day. And most encouragingly, this healthy energy flow doesn't necessarily depend on major architectural renovations or high financial investments; it depends, above all, on developing a new awareness of space, mindful attention to detail, and a willingness to make small, intentional changes. It's about observing the space with a new perspective, an energetic one, perceiving where energy seems to accumulate and become heavy, where it's clearly blocked by physical or symbolic obstacles, and where it dissipates rapidly without nourishing the environment.

A useful analogy often used in Feng Shui to understand Chi's behavior is to imagine it as water. Water, in its natural state, always seeks the easiest, most fluid paths, avoids insurmountable barriers (or patiently bypasses them), fills empty spaces in a balanced way, and brings life and fertility wherever it passes. However, when water is improperly dammed, blocked in its course, or wasted, it can cause floods, erosion, stagnation, and disease. The same principle applies to the vital energy of the house. If we block its main entrances – like doors that jam when opening, windows that remain always locked and closed, or large furniture placed in narrow passages right at the entrance – Chi loses its vital force upon entering the environment. If we allow broken, damaged, or energetically "dead" objects to occupy precious space – like stopped clocks symbolizing stagnant time, dusty artificial flowers representing false life, or unused electronic devices accumulating dense energy – Chi sickens, becomes heavy and contaminated. If we clutter environments with unnecessary excesses – furniture without a clear function, decorations without affective or aesthetic purpose, compulsive hoarding of things we don't use or love – Chi suffocates, loses its space to circulate and renew itself.

For this fundamental reason, one of the first and most powerful practices to restore the healthy flow of Chi in a home is the conscious and intentional release of what no longer serves. The famous "decluttering." The ideal home, from an energetic viewpoint, should contain only what has practical and frequent use, beauty that inspires, or deep affective meaning. Each object should deserve its place in the space, and each room should have a clear and defined function, aligned with the residents' needs and intentions. Air needs to circulate freely, light must be allowed to reach all corners, even the most hidden ones. And this should not be seen as a rigid, oppressive rule, but as a gesture of deep self-care, attentive listening to the space's needs, and commitment to one's own vitality and well-being. Releasing the old makes space for the new to flow into our lives.

While removing blockages, there are various ways to activate and strengthen Chi when it seems weak, slow, or insufficient in a particular environment. Living plants are extraordinary allies in this process: their mere presence attracts, moves, and renews the place's energy, symbolizing growth, vitality, and nature's strength. Small, well-maintained water features, with always clean and gently moving water, also powerfully revitalize the energy flow, especially when related to prosperity and financial flow. Natural crystals, like clear quartz, amethyst, or citrine, when cleansed and programmed with intention, can capture light, activate the energy of dark corners, and distribute positive vibrations throughout the environment. Soft, harmonious sounds – like calm instrumental music, the melodious tinkling of well-tuned wind chimes, or even the natural birdsong from outside – can awaken dormant energy, bringing lightness and joy. And natural, pure scents – from fresh or dried herbs, flowers, good quality incense, or essential oils diffused in the air – act as subtle breaths that renew and purify the home's energetic field, elevating the vibration and mood of the inhabitants.

Another crucial aspect to consider about Chi is its extreme sensitivity to human emotions. The vital energy of a space easily absorbs the feelings and thoughts that predominate in that environment. A house where frequent and intense arguments occur, where there's constant tension in the air, or where deep, unprocessed sadness resides, tends to absorb this denser vibration. Over time, even when the apparent conflict has ceased or the sadness has been partially processed, the space may continue to feel heavy, stuffy, charged, as if the walls themselves hold unresolved energetic echoes of those emotions. Therefore, besides regular physical cleaning, it's essential to also promote practices of energetic purification of the home (as we will see in detail later), using clear intention, gratitude, elements like salt, herb smoke, sound, or light, to renew the house's emotional field and release these subtle memories.

Attention to seemingly small details also significantly influences the quality and flow of Chi. The direction the bed faces, how one enters through the main door, what one sees immediately upon waking in the morning, the feeling when crossing a narrow or poorly lit corridor. Everything matters in Feng Shui. A well-placed mirror can visually expand a tight space and activate energy circulation; a beautiful, comfortable rug with harmonious colors can stabilize a room's energy, bringing coziness and security; a piece of art with vibrant colors and ascending shapes can uplift the environment's spirit and inspire creativity. Nothing is neutral in the energy field. Every choice we make in organizing and decorating our home subtly shapes the quality of the Chi we breathe there daily.

And this energy, once harmonized and balanced, reverberates positively in all aspects of our lives. Interpersonal relationships tend to become lighter and more fluid, with fewer conflicts and more understanding. The physical body responds with more vigor, disposition, and resilience. Thoughts organize with more clarity and focus. And even important life decisions seem to flow with less resistance, more intuition, and confidence. Living in a space with balanced Chi is like walking a path where the wind gently blows in your favor – there's less unnecessary effort, more pleasure in the journey, more presence in the moment.

It is also a profound way of respecting the "soul" of the house, its unique energetic identity, its history, its silences. By caring for the Chi, we care for this soul. We transform the house from a mere passive backdrop into an active, conscious ally. From a purely utilitarian space into a constant source of energetic and emotional nourishment. From a simple physical shelter into a true sanctuary for the spirit.

Vital energy is the invisible thread connecting the visible and invisible worlds, the material and the subtle. And when we learn to feel it, to listen to it with our body and intuition, and to guide it with intention and wisdom, the entire environment transforms. And with it, inevitably, our own life transforms too. Because there is no real separation between the quality of the space surrounding us and the quality of the energy pulsating within us. Where Chi circulates freely and harmoniously, the heart beats lighter. And where the heart beats light, everything naturally finds its proper place.

Chapter 5
Yin and Yang

The pulsating essence of the universe, in its incessant dance of creation and transformation, manifests through two fundamental principles, seemingly opposite in their qualities, yet absolutely interdependent and complementary in their nature. Yin and Yang are not just archaic symbols of a distant and abstract Eastern philosophy; they are primordial dynamic forces that actively shape everything that exists – from the macrocosm, with the cycle of seasons and the movement of stars, to the microcosm of our daily lives, influencing our mood on a cloudy morning, the arrangement of furniture in our living room, or the deep silence of an empty room at night.

At the heart of Feng Shui practice, this millennial principle of Yin and Yang serves as the fundamental foundation for any and all spatial harmonization: the dynamic, fluid, and ever-changing balance between these two forces ultimately determines the well-being of spaces and, consequently, the health and harmony of their inhabitants. Understanding and applying this complementary polarity is key to creating environments that nourish rather than drain.

Yin, in its archetypal nature, represents night, fertile darkness, introspection, cold, humidity, softness, receptivity, depth, the welcoming shadow. It is present in moments of rest and quiet, in the silent, protected corners of the house, in soft, fluid fabrics that invite touch, in dark, cool, and soft colors (like deep blue, black, gray, pastels), in rounded, curved, and embracing shapes, in low, continuous sounds, in descending energy. It is the force that invites us to the necessary pause, to inner retreat, to restorative sleep, to silent contemplation, to the gestation of new ideas in the womb of quietude. It is the energy of the archetypal feminine, of intuition, of being over doing.

Yang, conversely, is the bright light of day, manifest action, expansive heat, extroversion, ascending vibration, the force projected outward. It manifests vibrantly in large, well-lit environments (especially by natural light), in bright, warm, stimulating colors (like red, orange, bright yellow), in cheerful, loud, rhythmic sounds, in straight lines, pointed and angular shapes, in hard materials and shiny surfaces, in constant activities and energetic visual stimuli. It is the force that drives action, communication, celebration, expression in the world. It is the energy of the archetypal masculine, of logic, of doing over being.

It is crucial to understand that neither Yin nor Yang is intrinsically "better" or "worse" than the other. Both are equally essential to the totality of existence, like the two sides of the same coin, or the inhalation and exhalation that make up a complete breath. Imbalance arises not from the presence of one or the other, but from the disproportionate excess or significant absence of one relative to the other, or from rigidity in their interaction.

A house excessively dominated by Yin energy can seem sad, gloomy, lifeless, charged with an atmosphere of melancholy, apathy, stagnation, and difficulty initiating projects or feeling enthusiasm for life. There might be excess humidity, little light, accumulation of old objects, and a general sense of heaviness in the air. Conversely, a home where Yang energy predominates uncontrollably becomes agitated, restless, stressful, potentially chaotic, with excessive visual and auditory stimuli, little capacity to offer true welcome and rest, leading residents to a state of nervous exhaustion and difficulty relaxing and regenerating.

The secret to a harmonious environment, therefore, lies in the fluid and balanced dance between both forces – in allowing Yin and Yang to coexist dynamically, to alternate according to the needs of the moment and the function of the space, to mutually sustain each other in a constant flow of transformation. Feng Shui acts precisely at this crucial point: its goal is to identify, through sensitive observation, where there is an excess of Yin or Yang in a given environment and what is lacking, and then introduce elements that restore the fluidity of this vital balance. It's not about seeking static neutrality, but harmonic dynamism.

A bedroom, for example, due to its primary function of rest, regeneration, and intimacy, should predominantly favor Yin energy – it needs to be a space that invites deep relaxation, surrender, inner silence.

Light, soft, cool colors (like blues, seafoam greens, lavenders, rosy beiges), natural and soft fabrics (cotton, linen), diffused and indirect lighting (lampshades, low-intensity lights), absence of electronic devices emitting blue light and disturbing electromagnetic fields (like televisions, computers, cell phones), calming scents (lavender, chamomile, sandalwood), and above all, silence and privacy are effective ways to strengthen Yin energy in this sacred environment. An excessively Yang bedroom, with vibrant colors, lots of light, large mirrors, or active devices, hinders restorative sleep and tranquil intimacy.

Conversely, a kitchen, a place for food transformation (Fire element), or an office, a space dedicated to mental activity and productivity, need a certain energetic dynamism, and thus should contain a higher proportion of Yang energy to support their functions. Good natural and artificial lighting (brighter, focused light), colors that stimulate appetite (in the kitchen, like yellows and oranges) or mental focus (in the office, like greens or more vibrant blues), objects bringing vitality and movement, space for active circulation, and perhaps even light, stimulating sounds (like energizing background music) can contribute to a balanced and functional Yang environment. An excess of Yin in these spaces could lead to slowness, lack of appetite, or procrastination.

The first step to consciously working with the Yin and Yang balance in your home is to develop the ability to observe the feeling each room conveys. Trust your bodily and intuitive perception. Are there spaces where you enter and immediately feel an inexplicable weight, sudden drowsiness, a sense that time has stopped there, that energy is stagnant? There's likely an excess of Yin in that place, perhaps due to lack of light, ventilation, dark colors, accumulation of objects, or old memories. On the other hand, are there environments in your house that are tiring just to be in, that seem to accelerate your thoughts, with lights too bright and direct, excessive visual information (many objects, complex patterns), constant or intermittent noises? In this case, Yang energy is likely exacerbated, creating an overstimulating and exhausting environment. The body and senses are extremely precise instruments for this subtle energy reading. You don't need to memorize complex theories – just learn to listen to the visceral experience of being present in each space.

Bringing the necessary balance between these two primordial forces can start with surprisingly simple and accessible gestures. A dark, damp, lifeless corner, clearly dominated by stagnant Yin, can gain Yang vitality with the introduction of a warm, directed light fixture, a plant with colorful, vibrant flowers, a decorative object in a warm color (red, orange), or even a strategically placed mirror to reflect light from a nearby window. A very Yang space, like an all-white kitchen with shiny surfaces and intense lighting, can receive touches of Yin to soften and welcome, through the inclusion of plants with rounded leaves, natural fiber baskets bringing texture and warmth, a soft rug under the table, or a light, flowing fabric curtain on the window. The secret lies in identifying what is imbalanced (whether by excess or lack) and offering the complementary element in the right measure, like an alchemist carefully adjusting the ingredients of their potion.

Shapes and materials are also intrinsic carriers of these Yin and Yang energies. Curved, sinuous, organic lines, velvety, soft, fluid textures, round or oval objects evoke the softness and receptivity of Yin. Straight, angular, pointed lines, hard, smooth, shiny surfaces, square or triangular objects invoke the assertiveness and dynamism of Yang. Balancing them in the composition of an environment is like composing a visual and tactile melody: one seeks to avoid both excessive monotony (too much Yin) and disturbing stridency (too much Yang), creating a harmonious symphony of shapes and textures that favors well-being and sensory comfort. A curved sofa (Yin) with geometric patterned cushions (Yang), a rustic wood coffee table (Yin) with a polished metal vase (Yang) on it – are examples of how these energies can dialogue.

The position of furniture, as already mentioned, can intensify or soften these forces within a room. A bed directly aligned with the door, receiving the energy flow abruptly, is in a position considered "attacking" or Yang vulnerable. Repositioning it so the door is visible, but not in the direct energy flow (the "command position"), brings more sense of protection, control, and consequently, more Yin quality to rest. A desk facing directly towards a wall can suppress the Yang flow of creativity and future vision; turning it towards a window with a pleasant view or towards an open space within the room can activate this expansive potential. Furniture arrangement is not just functional, it's energetic.

Colors, as vibrational tools, are another key element in modulating Yin and Yang. Feng Shui observes their influence not only aesthetically, but primarily energetically and emotionally. Warm colors like red, orange, vibrant yellow, hot pink are considered Yang – they energize, stimulate, warm, attract the eye. Cool tones like blue, seafoam green, violet, gray, black, and also pastels and light neutrals (white, beige) are predominantly Yin – they soothe, calm, refresh, promote introspection. Choosing the ideal color palette for each room means aligning the space's vibration with its primary energetic function. A social space like the living room, for example, generally benefits from a balanced combination of both energies: perhaps a sofa in a neutral, light color (Yin) with decorative cushions in shades of red, gold, or orange (Yang), creating a composition that stimulates conviviality and joy, but also invites coziness and relaxation.

The natural cycle of the day itself offers a constant lesson on the dance of Yin and Yang. In the morning, the Yang energy of the sun rises, activates nature, awakens us to action. Throughout the day, this energy reaches its peak. At dusk and during the night, the Yin energy of darkness and coolness arrives, inviting rest, regeneration, retreat. Consciously aligning our home with this cosmic cycle is a powerful harmonization practice. Opening windows and curtains in the morning to let in the sun and fresh air activates the home's Yang energy, bringing vitality to the start of the day. Closing curtains, reducing artificial light intensity, and opting for warmer, indirect lighting at dusk favors the gradual return of Yin energy, preparing the body and mind for nighttime rest. It's not just a matter of lighting or ventilation; it's a way of synchronizing the microcosm of our home with the macrocosmic rhythms of the universe, promoting deeper, more natural well-being.

Another fascinating aspect of this philosophy is the understanding that Yin and Yang are always in a dynamic process of transforming into one another. Day inevitably turns into night, activity culminates in necessary rest, bright light gives way to restful shadow. In the spaces of our home, this transformation can and should also happen. An office that is predominantly Yang during the day, with focused light and stimuli for productivity, can become a more Yin space at night, with soft light, quiet music, and perhaps a relaxing scent, allowing the mind to disconnect from work. A bathroom that is functional and neutral during the day can transform into a true restorative spa at night, with candles, essential oils, bath salts, and silence, inviting a moment of Yin self-care and introspection. This fluidity allows the house to accompany our different emotional states and needs throughout the day and life.

When we feel tired and need rest, we can consciously attenuate the environment's Yang elements (reduce lights, sounds, vibrant colors) and bring in more Yin qualities (coziness, silence, darkness). When energy is low and we need a boost, we can increase Yang stimuli with brighter light, more vivid colors, energizing music, or opening windows to the sun. Thus, the home becomes a living, responsive space that welcomes us in our various phases, that doesn't imprison us in a single vibration, but frees us to be who we need to be at each moment.

Yin and Yang also teach us about the fundamental importance of contrast for perception and balance. An entirely bright, white environment can become blinding, sterile, and tiring; an entirely dark, heavy environment can oppress and generate melancholy. Balance and beauty are achieved in harmonious variation: light and shadow dialoguing, full and empty spaces complementing each other, firm surfaces and soft textures coexisting. The house containing both principles in constant dialogue is the one that can adapt with more grace and resilience to the different phases of its residents' lives. Because life is made of days of retreat and silence (Yin), and also of days of celebration, movement, and expression (Yang). Wisdom lies in creating a space that welcomes and sustains all these nuances of human experience.

And more than that: when we learn to consciously observe and apply the principles of Yin and Yang in our external space, this subtle understanding begins to spill over into our inner life. We start to perceive more clearly that there are times to act (Yang) and times to wait and receive (Yin), that there is intrinsic value in rest and contemplation (Yin) as much as in productivity and action (Yang), that there is no light without shadow, nor shadow without light – both are integral parts of the whole. The house, then, becomes a silent master, teaching us daily about rhythm, cycle, acceptance, and balance.

Feng Shui, through the lens of Yin and Yang, invites us not to choose one over the other, but to realize that one only exists and has meaning thanks to the presence of the other. And that the beauty and fullness of life reside precisely in this continuous balance, in this dynamic dance where everything moves, alternates, complements, and mutually sustains. When our home manages to reflect this cosmic dance in its atmosphere, it becomes a mirror of the universe itself – and the home transforms into an intimate, welcoming constellation, where every star, every aspect of our life, has its right time to shine and its necessary time to rest in fertile darkness.

Chapter 6
Five Elements

Ancient and profound Chinese wisdom, contemplating nature and the universe's workings, did not perceive it as a fragmented set of isolated objects and phenomena. Instead, it saw it as a dynamic and intrinsically interconnected system, a living organism where everything is energy (Chi) in constant transformation, flowing and interacting in perpetual cycles. Within this cosmic system, five great archetypal forces, five primordial energetic qualities, were identified as shaping matter, temporal cycles (seasons, times of day), physiological processes, emotional states, and crucially for Feng Shui, the vibration and balance of the spaces we inhabit: Wood (Mu), Fire (Huo), Earth (Tu), Metal (Jin), and Water (Shui).

These are the Five Elements – understood not just as literal physical substances, but as distinct vibrational expressions of vital energy, manifesting in colors, shapes, materials, sounds, tastes, emotions, behaviors, and very practically, in the composition and harmonization of our environments.

Each of these five elements represents a specific type of energy, with its own qualities, characteristics, and correspondences. Wood is the energy of spring, birth, vigorous growth, expansion, flexibility, and creativity. It symbolizes the vital impulse that launches upward and outward, like the sprout breaking through the earth seeking light. It's associated with the color green (in its various shades) and also light blue, rectangular and vertical shapes (like columns or tall trees), materials like natural wood and bamboo, the sour taste, wind, the East direction, the Liver organ, and the emotion of anger (in imbalance) or assertiveness and planning (in balance). In space, it manifests in healthy, living plants, tall and slender furniture, wooden floors, bamboo objects, paintings of forest landscapes. It's the energy that drives new beginnings, promotes development, extends towards new horizons. An environment lacking Wood energy can seem stagnant, lifeless, lacking initiative, with difficulty in change and growth. To activate it balancedly, one can include a thriving plant, a vertical bookshelf, green or blue decorative objects, or a piece of art evoking expanding nature. However, excess Wood can lead to impulsivity, irritability, impatience, and dispersion.

Fire is the element of summer, heat, rapid transformation, passion, contagious joy, fame, and recognition. It's the energy that reaches its peak, shines intensely, warms, illuminates, and connects people. It's linked to midday, the South direction, the heart and small intestine, the emotion of joy (in balance) or euphoria and anxiety (in imbalance), the bitter taste. In space, it appears vibrantly through warm colors like red, orange, hot pink, purple; triangular, pointed, or star shapes; the literal presence of fire in lit candles, fireplaces; intense and bright lighting; objects evoking celebration and enthusiasm. It's the energy that warms relationships, promotes social visibility, stimulates action and celebration. An environment completely lacking Fire tends towards emotional coldness, isolation, lack of enthusiasm and motivation, apathy. Conversely, excess Fire can generate excessive agitation, impulsivity, stress, conflicts, anxiety, and even burnout. Good use of Fire at home can be achieved through specific touches: red cushions, decorative candles lit with intention, warm and directed lighting, or a piece of art with intense, vibrant colors, especially in the Success area (Fire Gua).

Earth represents stability, the center, maternal care, nourishment, security, and support. It's the element that sustains, welcomes, grounds, allows digestion and assimilation (both physical and mental). It's linked to late summer (dog days), the center (and also Southwest and Northeast directions), the spleen-pancreas and stomach, the emotion of worry or rumination (in imbalance) or empathy and trust (in balance), the sweet taste. In space, it manifests through earthy tones like beige, brown, ochre yellow, terracotta; square, low rectangular, or flat shapes; materials like ceramic, clay, earth, stones, crystals; heavy and solid objects; thick rugs. It's the energy that generates feelings of security, belonging, comfort, and stability. An environment poor in Earth can seem cold, unstable, insecure, lacking coziness, too "airy." By including Earth elements, like sturdy ceramic vases, a thick natural fiber rug, a solid wood coffee table, or painting a wall in terracotta, solidity, grounding, and nourishment are returned to the space. Excess Earth, however, can lead to stagnation, stubbornness, excessive weight, and difficulty in change.

Metal is the element of autumn, contraction, precision, mental clarity, organization, discipline, and refined introspection. It represents the ability to discern, define boundaries, cut excess, value beauty in structure and order. It resonates with late afternoon, the West direction (and also Northwest), the lungs and large intestine, the emotion of sadness or melancholy (in imbalance) or courage and righteousness (in balance), the pungent taste. In environments, it appears in colors like white, gray, metallic tones (silver, gold, copper, bronze); in circular, oval, or spherical shapes; in objects made of metal, minimalist sculptures, smooth and reflective surfaces, polished stones. It's the energy that organizes chaos, brings focus and discipline, promotes justice and clear communication. An environment lacking a balanced presence of Metal can be perceived as confusing, scattered, disorganized, without clear boundaries. Excess Metal, in turn, generates excessive rigidity, emotional coldness, distance, harsh criticism, and difficulty expressing feelings. Balance can be achieved with subtle, elegant touches – a metallic lamp with clean design, a golden frame on a picture, a decorative object in the shape of a sphere, or the strategic use of white and gray in combination with other elements.

Water, finally, is the element of winter, fluidity, adaptability, deep intuition, emotion, communication, and ancestral wisdom. It's linked to night, the North direction, the kidneys and bladder, the unconscious, the emotion of fear (in imbalance) or calm and wisdom (in balance), the salty taste. In space, it arises through organic, asymmetrical, wavy shapes; dark colors like black and deep blue; mirrored or reflective surfaces (glass, mirrors); the literal presence of water in fountains, aquariums, vases with water; fluid and shiny fabrics (silk, satin). It's the energy that connects worlds (internal and external, conscious and unconscious), allows adaptation to change, delves into the soul's depths, promotes the flow of communication and prosperity. A space without Water energy can seem superficial, dry, rigid, lacking emotional or spiritual depth. An excess of Water, however, can generate mental dispersion, emotional instability, a feeling of lack of control, excessive melancholy, or lack of boundaries. Small gestures like hanging a light fabric curtain that sways gently in the wind, including a small fountain with clean running water (especially in the Career or Prosperity area), using mirrors cautiously and intentionally, or adopting a palette with details in black or navy blue can activate this element harmoniously and beneficially.

Crucially, these five elements do not exist in isolation in the universe or in our homes. They constantly interact in dynamic cycles – primarily the productive (Sheng) cycle and the control (Ke) cycle. Understanding these cycles is vital for applying Feng Shui effectively.

In the productive cycle, each element nourishes and generates the next, creating a flow of support and continuity: Wood feeds Fire (wood burns and produces fire); Fire generates ash, which becomes Earth; from Earth, Metal is extracted (ores); Metal, when cooled (or on cold surfaces), condenses and attracts Water (dew formation); and Water, in turn, nourishes the growth of Wood (plants need water). This cycle represents creation, harmonious growth, mutual support. This cycle is used to strengthen an element that is lacking: if Fire is missing, add Wood; if Earth is missing, add Fire, and so on.

The control cycle (or destructive, though "control" is more appropriate as its function is to maintain balance) represents containment, regulation, setting limits so no element becomes excessive and dominates the system: Wood breaks through and consumes Earth's nutrients (like tree roots); Earth absorbs and dams Water; Water extinguishes Fire; Fire melts Metal; and Metal cuts Wood (like an axe). This cycle is not inherently negative; it is essential for maintaining the system's dynamic balance, preventing one element from growing uncontrollably and suppressing others. This cycle is used to weaken an element that is in excess: if there is excess Fire, add Water (which controls it); if there is excess Wood, add Metal (which controls it). There is also a weakening (Xie) cycle, where an element "tires" what produced it (e.g., Fire burns Wood until consumed), used for subtler adjustments.

Applying these principles in home harmonization is much more than simply decorating with colors or objects associated with each element. It's learning to read environments as complex energetic expressions, to feel which element predominates or is lacking in each space, and to use the cycles intelligently to restore balance. A room with excess metal elements (too much white, gray, metal objects, round shapes) can seem cold, impersonal, and even generate sadness, despite sophisticated decoration. Perhaps it needs a touch of Fire (a red cushion, a candle) to warm and control the Metal, or Wood (a plant, a green object) to bring vitality and soften rigidity. A kitchen heavily loaded with Earth (brown tiles, heavy dark wood furniture, square objects) might feel heavy and stagnant, perhaps needing a touch of Metal (shiny stainless steel utensils, white details) to bring organization and clarity, or Water (a glass vase with flowers, a detail in dark blue) to add fluidity and freshness.

The diagnosis is largely sensory and intuitive. How do you feel in that space? Does it energize you, calm you, irritate you, depress you? What colors, shapes, and materials predominate? With practice and attentive observation, one begins to perceive what's missing, what's excessive, what needs transformation for the environment to become more balanced and nourishing.

Ideal harmony reveals itself in the balanced diversity of the five elements. A home where all five elements are present in appropriate proportions and in harmonious dialogue is like a healthy body, where all organs function well; like a well-tended garden, where different plants coexist and flourish; like a river flowing serene and clear between firm, nourished banks.

Each element, in its essence, also represents a fundamental human need and psychological quality: the need to grow, express oneself, and be flexible (Wood); the need for passion, joy, and social connection (Fire); the need for stability, security, and nourishment (Earth); the need for order, clarity, and boundaries (Metal); and the need for emotional fluidity, intuition, and deep connection (Water). Neglecting or suppressing one of these elements in the external environment often reflects and reinforces a denial or imbalance of that same quality within ourselves.

By consciously incorporating the Five Elements into the space, one seeks not a rigid mathematical formula, but deep and sensitive listening. Observing how each corner of the house behaves energetically, how each object vibrates in resonance or dissonance with the whole, how each color affects mood and disposition. And, from this heightened perception, subtly and intentionally introducing what balances, nourishes, elevates the energy of the space and, consequently, the energy of those who live there. This is the true alchemy of Feng Shui – transforming matter into energy and energy into well-being, quality of life, harmony.

The house then becomes a dynamic organism, constantly adapting and dialoguing, where elements alternate, support, regulate each other. A place that breathes with the inhabitant, strengthening them in challenging times and welcoming them in moments of silence and retreat. Because when the space we inhabit reflects the wise and balanced dance of nature's elements, it ceases to be an artificial setting and becomes an integral part of nature itself. And living in harmony with nature is, ultimately, living in peace and harmony with oneself, recognizing that the same elements composing the universe also compose our body, mind, and spirit. Harmonizing the home is harmonizing the self. And when this happens, life flourishes – with roots firm in the Earth, heart burning like Fire, mind clear as Metal, emotions fluid as Water, and spirit expansive as Wood.

Chapter 7
Tao and Nature

In the silent, unfathomable origin of all that exists, before forms, names, and dualities, rests the mystery of the Tao. The Tao is not a conceptual idea that can be fully grasped by the rational mind, not a religious belief requiring blind faith, nor a philosophical doctrine with fixed rules to follow. The Tao is the nameless Way, the spontaneous, natural flow of existence in its purest, most primordial form, preceding any human language that attempts to capture it.

Taoist philosophy, with its profound and paradoxical wisdom, does not aim to explain the universe or dissect it into parts; it proposes something far more radical and transformative: learning to walk *with* it, to flow *along* with it, to dance in tune with its subtle and inevitable rhythms. To live according to the Tao is to live in deep harmony with the natural order of things, accepting with equanimity the inescapable cycles of life and death, the tides of time that bring and take away, the seasonal rhythms of nature manifesting within and outside us. And it is precisely this fundamental principle of fluidity, acceptance, and attunement with the natural that underpins the ancient art of Feng Shui and transforms the simple act of inhabiting a home into a mirror of the wisdom of the universe itself.

At the heart of Taoist thought lies the understanding that the human being is not, in any way, separate from nature – he *is* nature. The illusion of separation, the arrogant belief that we can control, dominate, and exploit the natural world without consequence, is seen as the root of much of the conflict, suffering, and imbalance we experience individually and collectively. When one resists the natural flow of things, tries to impose their narrow will upon space or others, attempts to force what does not want to be forced – be it a river to change course, a plant to grow out of season, or an emotion to be suppressed – the vital energy (Chi) stagnates, becomes blocked, sickens. But when one learns to live in sync with the blowing winds, the rising and setting light, the expanding heat and contracting cold, the welcoming shadow and flowing water, everything in life begins to unfold with more lightness, less effort, more grace. The Tao then reveals itself not as an external entity or personal god, but as a subtle direction, an internal alignment with the immanent intelligence of the cosmos itself.

Applying the principles of the Tao to the configuration and experience of our home does not, therefore, require any complicated esoteric techniques or specialized architectural knowledge. It requires, first and foremost, listening. Deep, patient, attentive listening, not just with the ears, but with the whole body, with all sensitivity. Listening to the space we inhabit is, in essence, listening to the Tao itself manifesting there. A room that remains chronically dark, where natural light never fully penetrates, may be asking for more openness, more connection to the outside, more Yang energy to balance the quietude. A long, narrow, stuffy corridor, where energy seems trapped, might be crying out for a breath, a point of light, an expanding mirror, a revitalizing change. A kitchen excessively lit by cold artificial lights at night might be preventing the body from relaxing and entering the rest mode necessary for good digestion and sleep. That ignored corner of the living room, where random objects accumulate seemingly without sense, could be symbolically speaking about neglected emotions, aspects of life we don't want to see or deal with. The physical space constantly whispers; the Tao teaches the art of hearing these whispers.

The Tao teaches through simplicity and naturalness. "Wu Wei" – one of the central and most paradoxical concepts of Taoism, often translated as "non-action" or "effortless action" – is the heart of Taoist practice applied to life. This does not mean inertia, passivity, or laziness, but acting in perfect harmony with the natural flow of things, without unnecessary effort, without forcing results, without fighting against the current. It's like the experienced sailor adjusting the sails to use the wind's force to their advantage, instead of rowing against it. In the home, this translates to accepting and valuing the environment's natural characteristics – its solar orientation, ventilation, original materials, history – instead of constantly fighting against them. A room receiving naturally soft, indirect light can be embraced and enhanced as a space for introspection, reading, and calm, rather than being forced to look like a super-bright, vibrant environment that doesn't match its intrinsic nature. A darker, more protected corner can become a perfect meditative nook, a place for silence and retreat, instead of artificially trying to transform it into the center of the home's social activities. Wu Wei is the art of working *with* existing energy, not *against* it.

This principle of naturalness also invites us not to project unnecessary excesses onto our spaces. Modernity, often driven by the logic of incessant productivity and the appeal of constant consumption, frequently imposes an aesthetic and functional anxiety on environments: every corner must be filled with something, every wall decorated with the latest trend, every square meter functionalized to the maximum. The Tao radically departs from this mentality of compulsive filling. It points, instead, to the beauty and power of fertile emptiness – the Japanese "Ma" – to the space *between* things, to the importance of what is unseen but allows the visible to exist and breathe. An environment with free space for circulation, with walls that can breathe, with areas of visual "emptiness," is like the silent pause in a melody – it is this pause that allows the music to be appreciated, that allows for breath, contemplation, inspiration. Emptiness is not absence; it is potentiality.

Nature, in its complexity, simplicity, and perfect cycles, is the supreme model of the Tao in action. Therefore, a house seeking alignment with the Tao inevitably reconnects with the natural world, even if located in the heart of a city. This doesn't require having a forest nearby or a privileged sea view. It means developing the sensitivity to observe the dance of daylight through the windows, the shadows moving slowly across the walls throughout the hours, the subtle direction of winds entering and leaving, the living texture of wood under the fingers, the way rain gently taps the window creating an ephemeral melody. It means cultivating the habit of placing bare feet on the floor to feel the temperature and texture of the earth or the flooring, feeling the warmth of the morning sun entering through the window and warming the skin, perceiving the coolness settling in the air during the night. It's bringing consciousness back to the senses, to the direct, unmediated experience of the environment.

In practice, integrating the Tao into the home might mean, for example, valuing and respecting the natural solar orientation of rooms when deciding their functions. A room facing East, receiving the first morning sun, can be excellent for waking up gently with renewed energy. A resting or reading area facing West can be blessed by the golden, tranquil light of the setting sun, inviting calm and reflection. It's not necessarily about forcing structural changes in the house, but about aligning the *use* of spaces with the natural energy they intrinsically possess, observing how light and temperature vary throughout the day and seasons.

Respect for nature also manifests profoundly in the choices of materials for construction and decoration. The Tao favors the natural, the simple, the authentic, the essential. Natural fiber fabrics like cotton, linen, or hemp, which breathe and allow energy exchange with the body. Wood that ages with dignity, showing its marks and history. Hand-molded ceramics, with irregularities telling of the human touch. Stones carrying the geological memory of time in their veins and textures. It's not ostentatious luxury or industrial perfection that defines a Taoist environment, but authenticity, the honesty of materials. The object revealing its origin, function, and intrinsic nature is considered more valuable and energetically richer than one hidden under synthetic varnishes, imitations, or excessively polished finishes. True beauty, for the Tao, arises from direct contact with the real, with what is genuine.

    This Taoist view of space also teaches us about the virtue of humility. The house is not entirely at our disposal as a stage for status display or an object to be controlled and modified at our whim. It is an extension of the natural world, a living organism with which we cohabit. And as such, it deserves reverence, respect, listening. Just as the wise gardener observes the earth, feels its moisture, analyzes its composition before planting a seed, the conscious inhabitant observes the house, feels its energy, perceives its natural flows before intervening drastically. The Tao is against arbitrary imposition – it favors subtle adjustment, patient listening, flowing together. Therefore, before decorating impulsively, organize what already exists. Before painting a wall, deep clean the space. Before adding new objects, remove what is excessive or no longer functional. This is the rhythm of nature itself: creating from the essential, pruning to strengthen, emptying to renew.

The Tao also reveals itself in the flow of time. A living house, like an organism, constantly changes. And the Tao teaches the art of not clinging excessively to past forms, of accepting impermanence as an intrinsic part of existence. There are times when it's necessary to empty a room, let go of objects that have completed their cycle, move furniture to create new configurations, change colors that no longer resonate with the present moment. Not due to superficial fads or fleeting boredom, but because the energy of the place has changed, because one cycle has ended and another needs to begin. Something in you has profoundly changed, so the house also needs to change to reflect and support this new phase. Just like the seasons of the year, which ask no permission to transform into one another, the house also has its cycles of renewal. Living with the Tao is accepting that your house today doesn't need to be – and probably won't be – the same as yesterday. And that your life doesn't need to either. Change is the only constant.

This philosophy extends to the simplest daily habits. How does one walk through the house – hurried and distracted, or with conscious, present steps? How are objects touched – carelessly or with reverence? How is food prepared – mechanically or as a ritual of nourishment? The Tao is potentially present in every gesture. Lighting a candle with presence and intention. Opening a window in the morning with gratitude for the light and air. Sitting on the floor for a few moments and just listening to the sound of the wind outside or the silence inside the house. Small actions charged with mindfulness transform banal routine into sacred rite, physical space into living temple, fleeting moment into portal to eternity.

The house, then, ceases to be just a physical structure of bricks and mortar and becomes a living, pulsating inner landscape, full of meaning. And you, more than a mere resident or owner, become an active, conscious participant in this delicate energetic ecosystem. Each room becomes an element of your vast inner world. Each object plays a role in the subtle theater of your personal energy. Each light turned on or off is like a sun rising or setting within you, marking internal cycles.

Living with the Tao is fundamentally abandoning the exhausting effort to control everything. It's cultivating trust in life's intrinsic intelligence. It's realizing that nature already knows what it's doing – that the wind already blows where it should blow, that light already enters where it needs to enter, that silence has its own deep wisdom to offer, that things often resolve themselves when we stop trying to force them. And when our home aligns with this basic trust in the flow of existence, everything gains a new coherence, a new harmony. The body relaxes more deeply, the chattering mind quiets more often, the heart opens more easily to the beauty of the present moment. And thus, the Tao ceases to be just a distant philosophical idea and becomes concretely embodied in the house, in the way it breathes, welcomes, silently transforms us. Because the Tao, in its ultimate essence, is the primordial home of all things, the source from which everything emerges and to which everything returns. And by making your house a conscious reflection of this eternal principle of natural harmony, you are not just decorating a physical space – you are, finally, learning to inhabit, with reverence and joy, your own essential nature.

Chapter 8
Wabi-Sabi Aesthetics

There's a form of beauty that doesn't announce itself loudly, that doesn't seek dazzling brilliance or impose itself through perfect symmetry or grand forms. It doesn't reside in mathematical perfection but subtly blooms in the natural wear caused by time and use. It's not found in what was mass-produced to impress the masses but reveals itself in the uniqueness of what has been lived with sincerity, carrying the marks of history on its skin. This discreet, deep, melancholic, yet serenely joyful beauty has a name echoing Japanese wisdom: Wabi-Sabi.

Intrinsically linked to Zen Buddhism and the tea ceremony, this aesthetic philosophy far transcends simple interior decoration – it is, fundamentally, a way of looking at the world, a way of gracefully accepting the impermanence of all things, revering the beauty contained in the imperfect, the unfinished, the modest, and finding a deep, silent charm in what time has touched with its gentle patina.

While much of Western aesthetics historically pursues exact forms, straight and precise lines, smooth and polished surfaces, flawless finishes, and the eternal youth of materials, Wabi-Sabi deliberately celebrates traces of imperfection, the beauty of natural asymmetry, the irregular texture inviting touch, the suggestion of incompleteness opening space for imagination. A handmade ceramic cup with a slight defect on the rim, a solid wood table with marks left by glasses and conversations over the years, an old linen cloth that has lost its original stiffness and gained a welcoming softness – all these elements, under the sensitive gaze of Wabi-Sabi, are not seen as flaws to be corrected or discarded, but as precious testimonies to the passage of time, human interaction, the life that happened there. They are scars that tell stories, signs that the object was used, loved, integrated into the dance of existence.

Bringing this worldview into our home is a gesture of profound reconciliation with the inescapable truth of existence: everything is transient, everything changes, everything passes, everything ages. Wabi-Sabi gently invites us to stop fighting against this impermanent, fluid nature of things – and of our own lives – and to finally embrace it with acceptance and even appreciation. The house, then, ceases to be a static setting we try to freeze in time, a stage of unattainable perfection, and becomes an organic space that breathes with time, visibly transforms with daily use, carries and honors the history of those living there in its very surfaces and structures. Accepting the marks of time in the house is accepting the marks of time in ourselves.

In physical space, Wabi-Sabi aesthetics clearly manifests in the conscious choice for natural, authentic materials that reveal their origin and essence. Raw wood or wood with minimal finishes allowing its texture and grain to be felt, stone in its raw state or simply shaped, baked clay retaining the warmth of the hands that molded it, iron poetically rusting with time and humidity, rustic fabrics like linen, hemp, unbleached cotton, lime or clay walls that breathe and change hue with light, antique or second-hand furniture carrying marks of time and stories of other lives are valued. It seeks everything that carries memory, everything that tells a silent story of use and affection. It doesn't primarily seek the new, the shiny, the mass-produced, but the authentic, the singular, what has soul. It doesn't chase the unattainable ideal of perfection but values the essential, the simple, the functional with intrinsic beauty. Every object, under this peculiar gaze, gains new dignity.

That old chair inherited from grandparents, gently creaking when someone sits, is not seen as an annoyance to be fixed or replaced, but as a tangible link to the past, a sound bridge connecting generations. The ceramic vase broken in an accidental fall and carefully glued with a special resin, perhaps even with gold powder (in the *kintsugi* technique), far from being discarded as useless, becomes a powerful symbol of repair, resilience, acceptance of the break's history as part of the object's beauty. There is deep beauty in the survival of things. There is silent poetry in matter continuing to exist, transformed, even after fracture, loss, wear. Scars, in Wabi-Sabi, are not hidden; they are celebrated as part of the object's unique identity.

This philosophy of accepting imperfection and the passage of time also teaches us, paradoxically, about the importance of detachment. Because, by deeply recognizing that everything is transient, that nothing lasts forever in its original form, it becomes easier and more natural to let go of what has completed its cycle in our lives, what no longer resonates with who we are in the present. The Wabi-Sabi house is not a full house, cluttered with objects accumulated out of attachment or fear of scarcity. On the contrary, it immensely values empty space, visual silence, the interval between things allowing each element to breathe and be appreciated in its uniqueness. Each piece that remains has its defined place, not by rigid aesthetic convention, but by its intrinsic meaning or essential function. What no longer serves the current purpose of life, what no longer brings joy or utility, departs with gratitude for the service rendered. What remains has deep meaning. The essential is sufficient.

The color palette in Wabi-Sabi aesthetics naturally tends towards the neutral, the muted, derived directly from nature in its more sober and earthy tones. Shades of gray reminiscent of stones and clouds, browns of earth and aged wood, beiges of sand and dry fibers, moss or olive greens, grayish blues like the sky before a storm. These are colors that don't scream for attention, don't compete for the eye, but gently welcome vision, creating an atmosphere of calm, introspection, and repose. Light is also treated subtly – natural light is preferred whenever possible, perhaps filtered through light fabric curtains or rice paper panels (*shoji*), creating soft, shifting shadows. Artificial lighting is used sparingly, usually with warm color temperature (yellowish), diffused, indirect, like the light from a paper lantern or a candle, suggesting more than revealing, leaving areas in penumbra, inviting mystery and quietude. Excess is not used, neither for lighting nor decorating. Everything is minimal, essential, but never cold or sterile. It is the minimum that possesses soul, carries human warmth and history.

Wabi-Sabi is also intrinsically about the relationship with time. Time not as an enemy to be fought with anti-aging products and restorations erasing history, but as a silent, wise sculptor of objects, surfaces, emotions. A house aging with dignity, showing its marks without shame, is a house that has lived, been a stage for stories, accumulated experiences. The wooden floor worn in high-traffic areas, where feet always tread the same path. The drawer pull that has lost its original shine from repeated hand touches. The cushion gently deformed by constant use, molding to the body resting there. All these are precious testimonies of coexistence, of interaction between human beings and their environment. Nothing needs to look perpetually new, as long as it is clean, functional, whole in its essence, and above all, loved.

This deep respect for time naturally extends to practices of caring for the house and its objects. Maintenance, repair, conservation are valued over easy disposal and constant replacement. What can be restored with care and intention is not thrown away. An object is not automatically replaced just because it shows signs of use. Wabi-Sabi care is a gesture of loving, patient attention to what already exists, a recognition of the intrinsic value of things that serve us. Sewing a small tear in fabric. Gently sanding wood to reveal its beauty beneath the surface layer. Rewaxing an antique piece of furniture to nourish and protect it. And by doing so, not only is the lifespan of objects prolonged – the affective bond we have with them is also prolonged, deepening the relationship and shared history.

Wabi-Sabi is equally a profound lesson in humility and simplicity. Nothing in a Wabi-Sabi environment is made to flaunt wealth, status, or power. There is no apparent luxury, no flashy design, no excessively expensive or rare materials. Luxury, if it exists, resides in the invisible: in the quality of time shared in that space, in the affective memory accumulated in objects, in the simplicity achieved through detachment from the superfluous. A handmade tea bowl by a local potter, with a slight imperfection in shape or glaze, carries much more truth, beauty, and Wabi-Sabi energy than an industrially perfect object, mass-produced and soulless. Because it was made by someone, with intention and human touch. Because it is unique in its nuances. Because it lives and breathes through its imperfect materiality.

This particular way of inhabiting space naturally aligns with a calmer, more contemplative state of mind. Those who consciously adopt Wabi-Sabi aesthetics within their home tend also to adopt a calmer pace of life, a keener appreciation for the small things of everyday life, sincere gratitude for what simply *is*, here and now. The moment of preparing and drinking a cup of tea becomes a ritual of presence. The silence of the night becomes welcoming and fertile, not threatening. The task of tidying the house transforms into a form of moving meditation, a contemplation of objects and space. It's not about doing *more* things – it's about being *more present* in what already is.

From the energetic perspective of Feng Shui, Wabi-Sabi aesthetics significantly contributes to spatial harmony because it reduces visual and emotional noise. Environments loaded with new, flashy objects, excessive shine, vibrant colors, and aggressive angles tend to cause constant sensory excitement, accelerating the mind, fragmenting attention, and requiring continuous processing effort. Conversely, a house with simple, meaningful objects, soft natural colors, organic shapes, and the tranquil marks of time invites internalization, silence, deep listening to the senses and the heart. It's a house that welcomes the soul, rather than demanding from or agitating it.

Wabi-Sabi aesthetics also naturally contribute to the balance of the Five Elements. Earth (through ceramics, stone, earthy colors), Wood (natural wood, bamboo, plants), and Water (fluid shapes, subtle dark colors, impermanence itself) are especially valued and frequently present. Fire (warm colors, intense light) and Metal (shine, formal perfection, straight lines) tend to appear more subtly, restrained, without dominating the composition. The result is generally a more centered, introspective environment, with predominantly Yin energy, but in a balanced, fluid, and gentle way.

And more than anything else, perhaps the greatest lesson of Wabi-Sabi is about radical acceptance.

Accepting the house as it is, with its cracks, marks, history. Accepting life as it presents itself, with its cycles of joy and sorrow, gain and loss. And, fundamentally, accepting oneself at the exact point on the path where one stands, with all imperfections, scars, and unique beauties. The small crack appearing unexpectedly on the wall doesn't need to be hidden with urgency and shame – it can be seen as a timeline, a natural record of the house's life. The water ring left by a forgotten glass on the wooden table can be the silent record of a pleasant afternoon conversation with someone dear, an affective memory imprinted on matter. Everything is memory. Everything is testimony. Everything is part.

By consciously inhabiting a house breathing Wabi-Sabi, one reconciles with time, with silence, with the humble beauty of the everyday, with one's own imperfect and transient being. One learns that true beauty is not something imposed from outside, but something emerging from within, from authenticity, simplicity, acceptance. And that deep harmony lies not in hiding or denying what is imperfect, but in welcoming it with reverence, with curiosity, even with tenderness. Because, deep down, it is the same with us, human beings. We are made of marks of time, folds in the soul, imperfections telling our unique, unrepeatable story. And if there is beauty in all this – and Wabi-Sabi assures us there is, and plenty – then there is beauty in every house that simply lives. In every object that has withstood time and use. In every corner that has seen the sun rise and set countless times. Wabi-Sabi reminds us, with its discreet elegance, that it doesn't take much to live well – just eyes that know how to see beauty where it hides. And a heart willing to find fullness and charm where the world, hurried and obsessed with perfection, often only sees wear, flaw, or end.

Chapter 9
Zen and Space

In the pulsating heart of Japan, amidst the ethereal aroma of tea, the whisper of wind dancing with bamboo leaves, and the firm cadence of steps on tatami, a unique philosophy blossomed, a silent art of inhabiting silence: Zen. This spiritual path doesn't announce itself loudly, doesn't strut in showcases, nor impose itself with dogmas. Zen simply is; it resides in the subtle intervals between daily gestures, in the reflective pause separating words, in the deep quietude revealed when the superfluous is gently set aside.

This stream of thought, rooted in Buddhism, transcended the sphere of the Eastern mind to also shape the perception and configuration of spaces. Its mere mention has become almost synonymous with serenity, mental clarity, and a peace that seems to emanate from the very walls.

The essence of Zen lies in a radical, almost stark simplicity. This simplicity should not be confused with absence or sterile emptiness; it is, in fact, a form of limpid, unobstructed, essential presence. This principle permeates traditional Japanese architecture, the meticulous organization of rooms, and even the way one walks within the house, with conscious, reverent steps.

The Zen space does not aim to impress the senses with opulence or complexity. Its purpose is different: to dissolve. To dissolve the haste that quickens the heart, the mental confusion that clouds discernment, the incessant noises of the world that disconnect us from ourselves. It extends a silent invitation to the body to truly rest, to the breath to deepen and find its natural rhythm, to the gaze to quiet down, finding beauty in what simply is.

This subtle invitation is made not through an accumulation of objects, however beautiful, but paradoxically, through their calculated absence, through the careful curation of what remains. The well-known minimalist precept "less is more" finds its most refined and spiritually significant expression in Zen. A house inspired by this philosophy does not fill itself with superfluous adornments; it carefully empties itself of visual and mental distractions. Every object that remains has a clear reason for being there, a defined function, a story that resonates with the resident's soul. Every architectural line, every choice of material, every intentional void respects and promotes lightness of mind, clarity of spirit. There is visible space between the few carefully chosen pieces of furniture, there is space on the walls that breathe without excess pictures, there is space in the closets where things are not crammed. It is precisely in this physical space, in this *Ma* – the Japanese concept for the interval, the significant void – that inner silence finds conditions to breathe, to manifest. In Zen, physical space is not randomly filled with things; it is inhabited by pure intention.

A single vase containing a solitary flower, arranged with care and mindfulness (*ikebana*), can hold more meaning and beauty than an exuberant arrangement. A tatami mat spread on the floor transforms the floor into a stage for the present moment, an invitation to dignified posture, sitting or lying. A meditation cushion (*zafu*) on the light wood floor is not just a seat; it is a portal where the body rests and the mind quiets to listen to what truly matters. Lighting, a crucial element, is almost always diffused, subtle, as if emanating from within the walls themselves through rice paper panels (*shoji*), filtering external light and creating an atmosphere of softness and introspection. Permitted sounds are minimal, natural: the almost imperceptible creak of wood working with time, the rhythmic dripping of water in a bamboo fountain (*shishi-odoshi*) in the garden, the slight rustle of a linen fabric in the open window.

This pared-down aesthetic is profoundly functional, allowing life to flow without obstacles. However, it is also profoundly spiritual, as Zen understands that the external environment is a direct, almost immediate reflection of the state of mind. A disordered house, crammed with objects, full of material excesses, inevitably activates and amplifies internal noise, mental agitation, latent anxiety. Conversely, a clear, clean house, free of physical and visual obstructions, naturally leads to a meditative state, clarity of thought, inner peace. The home, from this perspective, ceases to be just a physical shelter to become a daily temple. Not a temple in the strictly religious sense, with dogmas and fixed rituals, but a sacred place for practicing mindfulness, where every act – sweeping the floor, washing dishes, sitting for tea – can be a form of moving meditation.

Zen design favors predominantly horizontal lines. They broaden the gaze, create a sense of stability, calm visual perception, contrasting with the often agitated verticality of the outside world. Chosen colors are invariably natural, drawn from Earth's own palette: various shades of gray reminiscent of river stones, beiges suggesting dry sand, whites evoking snow or clouds, light wood in its original tone, and black used sparingly, as a counterpoint, as the necessary shadow to light. Textures also refer to nature in its purest state: the gentle roughness of stone, the organicity of wood not overly treated, the translucency of rice paper, the breathable weave of raw cotton, linen. The shapes of objects and furniture are simple, pure, devoid of unnecessary ornaments, focused on the essence of function and the beauty of the line.

The result of this careful combination is a space where the gaze can rest without being captured by excessive details, where vital energy (Chi or Ki) can circulate smoothly, without blockages, and where the mind finds a natural resonance with calm, silence, fertile emptiness. It is important to note that this pursuit of simplicity does not aim to create a sterile, cold, or impersonal house. Zen does not seek emptiness for emptiness's sake, absence for absence's sake. It seeks fertile emptiness, the potential space where something genuine can happen, where contemplation can arise spontaneously, where the essential, so often suffocated by excess, finally reveals itself. Every object chosen to inhabit this purified space must possess soul, must tell a silent story. An old iron kettle with the indelible marks of time and use (*Wabi-Sabi*). A poetry book resting on the low table not as decoration, but as a constant invitation to reflection. A solitary plant, perhaps a bonsai or bamboo, establishing a mute, deep dialogue with the changing light entering through the window.

This way of inhabiting, so focused on the essential and the present, also requires another way of living, a corresponding inner posture. Zen invites a conscious slowing down of modern life's frantic pace. It invites cooking with mindfulness of each ingredient, each cut, each aroma. Washing dishes not as a chore, but as a ritual of cleansing and purification. Sitting with an erect spine, whether on a meditation cushion or a simple chair, and observing the light changing its hue and direction throughout the day. In this context, everything can become spiritual practice. Everything can become a path of self-knowledge. The physical space then becomes a faithful mirror of the consciousness that inhabits and animates it.

Creating a small meditation corner within the home is one of the clearest and most accessible expressions of this philosophy in daily life. No grand apparatus or investments are needed. A comfortable cushion on the floor, perhaps on a natural fiber rug. A lit candle symbolizing the light of consciousness. Perhaps incense with a soft, natural scent to purify the air and elevate vibration. An image inspiring serenity – a landscape, an abstract symbol, a spiritual figure, or simply the empty wall. More important than the aesthetics of this corner is the use made of it. Let it be a place reserved for pausing. For breathing consciously. For listening to one's own being beyond the noise of thoughts. This corner of silence, even if small, becomes a core of peace that gradually radiates its serene influence to the rest of the house.

Energetically, Zen philosophy aligns almost perfectly with the fundamental principles of Feng Shui. Both seek the free, harmonious flow of vital energy, clarity in forms and organization, the dynamic balance between Yin (rest, shadow, softness) and Yang (action, light, vigor) forces, and harmony among natural elements. A space conceived under Zen inspiration is, by its nature, energetically harmonious. It doesn't require many complex energetic corrections or cures, as it is already, in its conception, consonant with life's subtle laws, with the universe's natural flow.

There is, in Zen, a deep reverence for time and impermanence. The house is not seen as a static stage to display constant novelties, but as a living field of presence, where the past is honored, but not imprisoning, and the future is welcomed, but not generating anxiety. The old, inherited piece of furniture coexists peacefully with the newly painted neutral wall. The small imperfection in wood or ceramic is not hidden or discarded – it is accepted, sometimes even celebrated as part of the object's history, as testimony to the passage of time (*Wabi-Sabi*). The natural aging of materials is seen as part of the integral and beautiful process of life. Just as the people living there change, mature, quieten with age, the house also transforms, gains patina, tells stories on its surfaces.

And this silence charged with time becomes eloquent, deep. A Zen house doesn't need to shout from the rooftops that it is beautiful. It simply is. Not because it follows a fleeting decoration trend, but because it reflects a mind at peace with itself. True beauty, after all, always arises from inner peace, from serenity expressed externally. From sobriety that does not bore, but invites contemplation. From order that does not oppress, but frees the mind. From the essential that does not tire the eye, but nourishes it.

Transforming a conventional space into a Zen-inspired space does not necessarily require major structural renovations or hefty financial investments. It requires, first and foremost, an internal process of detachment, clarity, and intention. It begins with the courage to choose what stays and what goes. With the discipline to eliminate what occupies physical and mental space without real purpose. With the decision to let natural light in and air circulate. With the gesture of opening physical space so that inner space can expand. It requires cleaning with presence, not automatically. Moving the few remaining pieces of furniture carefully, feeling their weight and place. Inhabiting every corner with reverence, as if treading sacred ground.

At the end of this process, which is continuous, the house ceases to be just a place where one lives mechanically – it becomes a place that sustains conscious life. Every step taken within it is a step on the spiritual path. Every silent corner becomes an invitation to deep breathing, to regenerative pause. Every silence lingering within it echoes the primordial silence of being, that place of peace existing beyond thoughts and emotions. Living in a Zen space is, in essence, living with fewer things, but with more depth. It is exchanging material and sensory excess for the essence of being and living. It is allowing the environment itself to become a silent master, teaching about impermanence, simplicity, and mindfulness. It is making the everyday, with its simple gestures, transform into a continuous meditation. Because, ultimately, Zen is not a philosophy to be merely thought about or discussed – it is an experience to be lived, felt, embodied. And space, when attuned to this experience, becomes a living poem written in wood, air, light, and shadow. A poem needing no words to communicate its message. Because it already says everything with its eloquent silence, its calm and limpid presence. It is peace itself manifested in the form of home.

Chapter 10
Vastu Shastra

Long before the principles of Feng Shui began to be whispered in the mountains of China, an even older wisdom flourished in the vast and mystical land of India. There, grand temples and humble dwellings were designed and built based on a sacred science of space known as Vastu Shastra. This ancestral knowledge is not just an architectural system or a construction guide; it is, in essence, a profound spiritual science that investigates and harmonizes the relationship between human beings, their habitat, and the cosmos.

The very etymology of the term reveals its depth: the Sanskrit word "Vastu" refers to the site, the dwelling, the physical structure we inhabit, while "Shastra" means scripture, treatise, science, or revealed knowledge. Vastu Shastra is, therefore, the ancient treatise on the correct, harmonious, and auspicious way to inhabit earthly space, living in tune with universal laws and the cosmic energies that permeate us.

With roots delving deep into the Vedas – the millennial sacred texts forming the basis of Hindu tradition and much of Eastern philosophy – Vastu carries profound and detailed knowledge about the invisible yet powerful interconnection between the microcosm (the human being and their home) and the macrocosm (nature and the universe). At its philosophical core, Vastu starts from the fundamental conviction that every place on Earth, every piece of ground, possesses its own soul, a unique energetic vibration, a subtle entity known as *Vastu Purusha*. This cosmic being, according to tradition, inhabits each plot of land, and its position and energy directly influence the lives of those who build or dwell there. When a structure is erected or a house organized without due respect for this soul of the place, without considering cardinal directions and natural energy flows, dissonance is created, an imbalance that can manifest in various aspects of the residents' lives – health, prosperity, relationships, peace of mind. Conversely, when the dwelling is aligned with the universal forces encoded in Vastu, a harmonious energetic bridge is established between Earth and sky, between the individual and the Whole, allowing vital energy, or *Prana*, to flow freely, nourishing and sustaining life in fullness.

Although often compared to Chinese Feng Shui due to the common goal of harmonizing spaces to promote well-being, Vastu Shastra has distinct characteristics and a particular approach. While Feng Shui primarily works with the dynamic flow of Chi (vital energy) in constant movement and adaptation, using tools like the Bagua Map to chart symbolic life areas onto the house plan, Vastu adopts a more geometric, structured, and, in a sense, fixed approach. Its principles are heavily based on precise orientation according to cardinal directions and on mathematical calculations and proportions considered sacred.

Instead of the Bagua, Vastu primarily uses the *Vastu Purusha Mandala* as its guide, a sacred square diagram graphically representing the cosmic entity (Vastu Purusha) lying on the land, with its head facing Northeast and feet Southwest. Each part of Vastu Purusha's body, aligned with specific sectors of the Mandala and consequently with cardinal and intermediate directions, governs different aspects of life and indicates the ideal location for each function of the house. Spatial orientation, therefore, is one of Vastu's master pillars.

Its doctrine teaches that each of the eight directions (North, South, East, West, Northeast, Southeast, Southwest, Northwest) carries a specific energy, governed by a particular deity and associated with a ruling planet, directly influencing distinct aspects of life and the house's functionality. The North (Uttara), for example, is associated with Kuber, the god of wealth, and the planet Mercury; it is considered extremely auspicious for finances, business, and opportunities, which is why the main entrance of the house is ideally facing this direction, or at least has significant openings in this sector. The East (Purva), linked to sunrise, the god Indra, and the Sun, represents the energy of life, health, knowledge, and rebirth; it is an excellent direction for secondary entrances, meditation or study places, or even the living room, where morning light can bathe the environment. The South (Dakshina), ruled by Yama, the god of death (or discipline), and the planet Mars, is considered a direction of intense energy that needs careful handling; it's recommended this sector be more closed, with thicker walls or fewer openings, and house less frequented rooms or those requiring solidity, like storage rooms or, in some cases, the head of the family's bedroom, provided other rules are observed. The West (Paschima), associated with Varuna, the god of waters (in the cosmic context), and the planet Saturn, is a direction linked to the end of the day, to retreat; it can house storage spaces, dining rooms (where the family gathers at day's end), or service areas.

Intermediate directions also hold great importance: the Northeast (Ishanya), ruled by Shiva and Jupiter, is the most sacred direction, linked to water, spirituality, meditation, and mental clarity – ideal for altars, prayer rooms, water features, or contemplative gardens; the Southeast (Agneya), of the fire god Agni and Venus, is the natural abode of the fire element, making it the perfect location for the kitchen; the Southwest (Nairutya), ruled by the demon Nairuti and the lunar node Rahu, commands the Earth element and stability, being ideal for the master bedroom, as it favors solidity and security, but requires care not to become heavy or stagnant; and the Northwest (Vayavya), of the wind god Vayu and the Moon, governs the Air element and movement, being favorable for guest rooms, garages, or light storage.

Besides the crucial importance of orientation, the exact center of the house or plot – called the *Brahmasthan*, the place of Brahma, the Creator – is considered the energetic heart of the residence, the point of cosmic balance. This central space should ideally remain free, open, clean, and well-lit, without obstructions like heavy walls, pillars, large furniture, bathrooms, or stairs. The Brahmasthan is the point where subtle energy from all directions converges and from where it distributes to the rest of the house. An obstructed or contaminated Brahmasthan compromises the vitality of the entire space, potentially causing feelings of heaviness, pressure, difficulty in decision-making, mental confusion, and even physical imbalances in residents. Keeping the center free ensures the energetic "lung" of the house can breathe.

The five fundamental elements of nature, the *Pancha Mahabhutas*, are also present and essential in Vastu, albeit with some nuances compared to the Chinese Feng Shui tradition. In Vastu, the elements are: Earth (Prithvi), Water (Jala), Fire (Agni), Air (Vayu), and Ether or Space (Akasha). Each of these elements has an ideal location within the house map, corresponding to cardinal and intermediate directions and their energetic qualities. Balancing these five elements in the environment is fundamental for health and well-being. Earth (solidity, stability) predominates in the Southwest; Water (fluidity, spirituality) in the Northeast; Fire (transformation, energy) in the Southeast; Air (movement, communication) in the Northwest; and Ether (space, connection) reigns in the center, the Brahmasthan. The correct distribution of house functions according to the location of these elements (kitchen in the Southeast, altar in the Northeast, master bedroom in the Southwest, etc.) is one of Vastu's central goals for creating an energetically balanced environment.

Vastu Shastra also shows meticulous concern for harmonious mathematical proportions, building symmetry, natural land slope (ideally lower in the North and East, higher in the South and West), correct staircase location (avoiding the center and Northeast), proper bathroom placement (ideally Northwest or West, never Northeast, Southeast, or center), wall and ceiling heights, and even room shapes (preferably square or rectangular, avoiding irregular shapes or cuts). Everything in the physical space is seen as a direct reflection of the order (or disorder) of universal energy.

However, this apparent rigidity does not mean impractical inflexibility. Vastu recognizes that not every house can be built or modified to perfectly follow all principles, especially in modern urban settings or existing constructions. Therefore, the science of Vastu also offers a vast repertoire of subtle corrections, energetic adjustments, known as *Vastu remedies*. These might include the strategic use of mirrors to correct cuts or expand areas, installation of water features in specific locations, placement of auspicious plants, use of energized crystals, application of corrective colors, installation of *Yantras* (sacred geometric diagrams) at specific points, or performing purification and energization rituals to harmonize what cannot be physically modified. Applying Vastu principles in already built houses and apartments is, therefore, perfectly possible and often surprisingly effective. Small furniture shifts to free the center or improve flow, changing the use of certain rooms to better align them with directions, careful placement of mirrors to "bring" light or energy to a deficient area, introducing water features in the Northeast to activate spirituality and prosperity, placing specific plants to absorb negative energies or activate auspicious sectors, or using objects made of specific metals (like copper in the Southeast to enhance Fire balancedly) can significantly restore the flow of *Prana* in the environment. What matters, as in all subtle energy practices, is the combination of technique with clear intention and a present heart in the harmonization gesture.

Another fundamental difference between Feng Shui and Vastu lies in Vastu assigning energetic qualities and influences not only to environments themselves but also considering the relationship between the residents' Vedic astrology (*Jyotish*) and the place they inhabit. According to this view, a spatial configuration ideal for one person based on their birth chart might be unbalanced or even harmful for another. This introduces an additional layer of personalization and complexity to the analysis, reinforcing the importance of sensitive listening to the space combined with deep self-knowledge and, ideally, consultation with an expert who can integrate these different layers of information.

Symbolically, Vastu Shastra sees the house as a miniature replica of the universe, a microcosm reflecting the macrocosm. The roof corresponds to the sky (Akasha); the floor, to the earth (Prithvi); the walls represent structure and boundaries, aligned with cardinal points; and the center, the Brahmasthan, is the connection point with the divine, the creative source. By building and inhabiting a space respecting this sacred cosmology, a home is created where the individual is in constant dialogue and resonance with the Whole. Every step taken inside the house aligns, symbolically, with planetary energies, qualities of directional deities, the dance of the five elements. Every daily action – sleeping in the correct direction, eating facing East, working with adequate light, meditating in the Northeast corner – becomes a sacred offering, an act of conscious participation in the cosmic order.

Additionally, Vastu philosophy highly values purity, order, and cleanliness in the environment. A disorganized house, with accumulation of useless or broken objects (clutter), blocks the flow of *Prana* and attracts negative energies. Excessive visual stimulation, accumulation of electronic devices (especially in bedrooms or the center), neglect of physical maintenance (cracks, leaks, peeling paint) – all disrupt Vastu and weaken the home's vital energy. Therefore, just as important as the correct position of walls and house orientation is the living presence of consciousness and care in every detail of daily life. The resident should care for the house as if caring for a sacred temple – because, in Vastu's view, it indeed is.

In contemporary practice, many people find benefits in using both systems – Feng Shui and Vastu Shastra – in a complementary and integrated manner. While Feng Shui can offer valuable tools for adjusting the subtle flow of Chi daily, balancing Yin and Yang energies in rooms, and working with life areas through the Bagua more flexibly, Vastu provides a deep map of cosmic orientation, an energetic structure based on universal principles, and a spiritual connection with the forces of nature and the cosmos. Together, these two millennial systems offer a holistic and comprehensive view of space as a powerful tool for self-knowledge and life transformation.

A house aligned with Vastu principles promises not just physical comfort or practical functionality. It favors *Dharma* – the right path of being, each individual's life purpose. It functions as a mirror of cosmic order, an energetic field where humans can constantly remember they are an integral part of something much larger, of a universal intelligence governing all that exists. And when the house becomes this constant reminder, living transcends merely completing tasks or achieving material goals: it becomes a continuous ritual of alignment between heaven, earth, and heart.

Vastu Shastra reminds us, with its ancestral wisdom, that it's not enough just to occupy a place in the world. One must inhabit that place with reverence, consciousness, and respect. Aligning walls, doors, and windows is not just an act of architecture – it's a sacred act of aligning body with spirit, physical space with the soul inhabiting it, the everyday with the eternal. And in this silent, profound alignment, everything in life finds better conditions to flourish.

Chapter 11
Attentive Observation

Before any genuine transformation can occur in a space, even before the impulse to move a piece of furniture or choose a new shade for the wall, there is a primordial, often forgotten step: the act of seeing. Truly seeing. This implies observing, feeling, listening to the space that surrounds us with a rare, whole presence, stripped of hasty judgments and the veils of habit. Most people move through the rooms of their own homes as if repeating a well-known route by heart, an automatic choreography devoid of soul and attention. The eye glides over accumulated disorder as if it were an integral and immutable part of the usual landscape. The resilient body gets used to the discomfort of poorly positioned furniture, an uncomfortable chair, and simply stops noticing the discomfort. The air might be heavy, charged, stagnant, but hardly anyone breathes attentively enough anymore to truly perceive its density or lightness.

Attentive observation emerges, then, as the fundamental first gesture of reconnection between the inhabitant and their habitat. It is the key that reopens a dialogue long interrupted by routine and distraction. To practice it, it's essential to slow down the internal rhythm. It's necessary to interrupt the autopilot that guides us through rooms without us really being present in them. It requires the courage to enter each environment – the living room, bedroom, kitchen, bathroom – as if stepping there for the first time. Like visiting an ancient, unknown temple full of mysteries to be unveiled. Like treading with bare, sensitive feet upon the sacred ground of one's own soul reflected in the space.

The proposed gaze here is not the technical eye of the architect or decorator, nor the objective eye of the scientist. It is a primarily sensory, intuitive, deeply emotional gaze. It's about developing the ability to perceive what the environment communicates, not through explicit words, but through its eloquent silences, its shadows, its lights, its arrangements, and its absences. That abandoned chair in a dark corner of the bedroom, accumulating dust and forgotten clothes, certainly says something about abandonment or procrastination. A corridor that is always blocked, dark, or full of obstacles holds a story of blockage or fear. An entirely empty wall that no longer inspires vitality, but apathy; a closet so crammed with things it seems about to suffocate – everything in the space has its own voice, a subtle message, if there is an internal willingness for attentive and patient listening.

The invitation, in this chapter, is for a true sensory immersion into the intimate details of the home. Try walking slowly through each space, feeling the floor beneath your feet. Make deliberate pauses before each window, observing the view and the incoming light.

Stand before each mirror, noticing not just your reflection, but what it reflects of the surrounding environment. Contemplate each main piece of furniture, feeling its texture, shape, history. Sit in different spots in the living room, bedroom, kitchen – places where you normally don't sit. Stay there for a few moments, in silence. Feel what these places provoke in your body: is there relaxation or tension? What memories or emotions do they awaken? What thoughts arise spontaneously? What physical or emotional tensions seem to accumulate in that specific area? Often, one discovers that it's not the environment itself that is "wrong," but rather the way it has been forgotten, neglected, ceased to be seen and felt in its entirety.

Light is invariably one of the first and most revealing things to observe attentively. What path does natural light take inside the house throughout the day? Which rooms are bathed in the soft morning light? Which remain more shadowed during the afternoon? Is there enough light for the activities performed in each room? Is the light appropriate for the space's function – too soft for a work area requiring focus, or an overly aggressive glare where rest and relaxation are sought? Natural light narrates the story of time within the house, connects the interior with cosmic cycles. Listening to it, observing its nuances and movements, is an act of respect for the space's solar rhythm and our own biology.

After light, the air. How does it circulate through the rooms? Is it renewed frequently or does it seem stagnant, stale? Are there windows opened regularly, allowing exchange with the outside? Does any specific room always smell of mold, humidity, accumulated dust, abandonment? Does the air have a balanced temperature, or are there very cold or very hot spots? Does it seem to dry the skin or weigh on the lungs when breathing more deeply? Pausing in each room and taking a few deep, conscious breaths is a powerful way to feel the quality of the vital energy, the *Prana* or Chi, dwelling there – or stagnating there, needing movement.

Also observe the sounds composing the home's auditory landscape. Are there constant, low-frequency noises that have become so normalized by the mind they are barely perceived consciously? Does the refrigerator vibrate non-stop? Does a ceiling fan click rhythmically? Does the incessant sound of traffic invade the living room or bedroom? Is the silence, when present, pleasant, welcoming, or uncomfortable, oppressive? Does the house sing soft melodies or scream with harsh noises? Are there specific corners where sound seems trapped, muffled, choked, lacking resonance? Or, conversely, are there points where the echo is startlingly empty and impersonal? The sound quality of the environment directly impacts the nervous system and emotional state.

Attentive observation must crucially extend to the organization (or disorganization) of objects. What is displayed on shelves, sideboards, tables? Are they things that still hold real meaning for you, provoke affection, inspire, or bring back good memories? Or are they just forgotten trinkets, accumulated out of habit, unwanted gifts, or symbols of phases now past? Does the coffee or dining table accumulate piles of papers, unread mail, random objects? Does the kitchen hold drawers full of rarely or never used utensils? Do the clothes stored in the closet still fit who you are today, or do they belong to a past version of yourself? Meticulous attention to these details reveals what daily habit cleverly hides: the excesses that suffocate, the voids crying out for meaningful filling, the symbols that have become obsolete and no longer represent your current truth.

A precious and revealing practice in this reconnection process is the "meditative tour" of the house. With a notebook or journal in hand, walk through each room slowly, as if exploring a new and sacred territory. Sit in different points of each room. Observe in silence for a few minutes. Allow yourself to feel. Then, note down everything that arises: physical sensations (heat, cold, tightness, relaxation), spontaneous thoughts, memories that surface, emotions that manifest (joy, sadness, irritation, peace). At this moment, the most important thing is not to judge, not to try to correct or fix anything yet. Just perceive. Just record. Just welcome what the space and your body are communicating. This deep, unfiltered listening allows understanding of what kind of energy each space currently carries – and, more importantly, what kind of energy it is subtly asking to be transformed, released, or nurtured.

The physical body is the most reliable compass on this observational journey. Where the body spontaneously relaxes, where breath flows easily, is generally where the space welcomes, where energy is balanced. Where the body contracts, where shoulders tense up, where inexplicable discomfort arises, there is something to be looked at more attentively, more carefully. Perhaps the wall color in that location is too heavy for the resident's sensitivity. Perhaps the furniture is disproportionately large for the room size, creating a sense of oppression. Perhaps circulation is blocked by poorly positioned furniture, impeding the natural flow of movement and energy. Or, often, what causes discomfort is a simple yet powerful accumulation of things – visible or hidden – preventing air from flowing freely and the mind from finding rest.

    Observing attentively also includes directing the gaze towards broken objects, things stopped in time, hidden in the back of closets or drawers. Clocks that no longer work, burnt-out light bulbs never replaced, jammed drawers requiring force to open, obsolete electronic devices stored "for someday." Each of these details, however small they seem in isolation, carries a significant energetic message. A stopped clock is a potent symbol of stagnant time, difficulty moving forward. A burnt-out bulb represents a dark area in life, an aspect not receiving light or attention. A locked or jammed drawer can mirror a repressed emotion, a guarded secret, something one doesn't want to access.

    For this profound reason, attentive observation transcends a mere aesthetic or organizational exercise. It reveals itself as a powerful existential diagnosis. The house, in its entirety – with its lights and shadows, accumulations and voids, beauty and wounds – is a direct and precise reflection of the internal state of its inhabitant. And by observing it with courage and honesty, without filters or justifications, one can see with surprising clarity where energetic blockages reside, unresolved emotional tensions linger, unconscious forgetfulness shapes daily experience. The home becomes a mirror. And the mirror, when viewed with clarity and compassion, transforms into a precious opportunity for healing, self-knowledge, and realignment.

The most important aspect in this initial observation process is not to rush to change, fix, or transform immediately. Before action comes understanding. One must first listen to the house as one listens to a wise old friend, who has much to say if given time and space. One needs to know what it truly needs. What it carries in its walls and objects. What it protects with its dark corners. What it can no longer bear to carry. Changing without listening risks repeating the same patterns of disharmony in a new guise. Transforming without perceiving the root of the problem is merely decorating the surface, without touching the essence.

For all these reasons, attentive observation, practiced regularly and deeply, is the sacred and indispensable first step in any journey of harmonizing home and life. It inaugurates a new, more intimate and respectful bond between resident and dwelling. A bond where mutual respect and conscious care replace haste, neglect, and automatism. Where every subsequent gesture – moving a sofa, choosing a new color, opening a window, donating an object – arises from deep listening and not from momentary whim or external influence. It is in this silent yet immensely powerful gesture of stopping, looking, and feeling that the process of renewal truly begins to happen. Before changing the house, change the way you look at it. Before altering objects, transform the perception of yourself. And when this internal change happens, when consciousness expands to include space as an integral part of being, everything inside and out begins to vibrate differently, more coherently, more alive. Because where there is true observation, there is presence. And where there is authentic presence, there is always the beginning of healing.

Chapter 12
Senses of Space

The house we inhabit is not merely a visual construction, a set of shapes, colors, and objects presented to the eyes. It is a living entity that dialogues with us through multiple channels, engaging all our senses in a constant, often unconscious dance. The house is also felt on the skin through its textures and temperatures, heard in its silences and noises, smelled in its subtle or strong aromas, touched on every surface our hands encounter. It is intensely alive in details that frequently escape purely visual analysis but profoundly shape the daily experience in invisible and decisive ways. Every space we occupy, every room we cross, incessantly communicates with the totality of our senses, awakening physical reactions, forgotten memories, emotional responses, and subtle perceptions that define our relationship with the environment.

Recognizing this complex sensory interaction means realizing that true environmental well-being, the genuine feeling of being "at home," is built not just on aesthetic appearance, but on creating a welcoming and balanced atmosphere. And this intangible atmosphere is, in essence, the silent orchestra of all our senses playing in harmony.

The gaze, although often dominant in our Western culture focused on the visual, represents only one gateway to the full experience of space. Vision guides us through the colors surrounding us, the shapes defining objects, the organization (or lack thereof) of the environment, the intensity and quality of light bathing it. It allows us to appreciate beauty, identify functionality, perceive order. However, even a visually stunning environment, decorated with impeccable aesthetic taste, can become deeply unpleasant if, for example, it has a persistent, unpleasant smell, is filled with a disturbing, constant sound, or if the predominant textures are cold, rough, or uncomfortable to the touch. Visual harmony alone does not guarantee well-being. To truly harmonize a space integrally, it's necessary to activate and refine a broader, more delicate sensory perception, including and valuing all senses as pathways of knowledge and connection with the home.

Smell, among the senses, is perhaps one of the most direct and primitive pathways to deep memory and the center of emotions. A simple scent, often unexpected, possesses the almost magical power to instantly transport the mind to forgotten childhood moments, calm agitated breathing in seconds, energize a tired body, or conversely, provoke intense physical and emotional unease. A house persistently smelling of mold, old grease accumulated in the kitchen, aggressive chemical cleaners, or dust can be a continuous source of discomfort and even health problems, even if the cause isn't consciously perceived by residents accustomed to these odors. On the other hand, natural, subtle, pleasant aromas, like the delicate perfume of fresh flowers in a vase, the characteristic smell of clean wood, the fragrance of dried herbs hanging, or the ethereal scent of good quality incense, create an invisible yet powerful layer of welcome, well-being, and spiritual upliftment.

Each room of the house can even have a specific scent reflecting and reinforcing its function and the intention placed upon it. In the bedroom, for example, scents like lavender, chamomile, or sandalwood are known to favor restorative sleep, calm, and introspection. In the living room, citrus scents like orange or bergamot, or warm spices like cinnamon, can promote positive energy, joy, and stimulate social interaction. In the kitchen, the comforting smell of spices being used, bread baking, or food prepared with affection strengthens affective memory and the primordial sense of home, of nourishment. In the bathroom, essential oils like peppermint, eucalyptus, or tea tree offer an immediate sensation of freshness, cleanliness, and purification. It's important to note that these beneficial aromas don't need to come exclusively from expensive candles or electric diffusers; often, they emanate naturally from living plants in the environment, fresh fruits arranged in a kitchen basket, aromatic herbs grown in the window, or the raw wood of furniture itself.

Hearing is another sense frequently ignored or underestimated in composing and harmonizing domestic environments. And yet, the sounds present – or absent – in a space significantly shape the mental, emotional, and even physical state of residents. The constant, often monotonous noise of operating electronic devices (refrigerators, air conditioners, computers), noisy fans, the persistent sound of traffic from the street, or even the television constantly on in the background, even without paying attention to it, can generate chronic muscle tension, mental fatigue, difficulty concentrating, and generalized anxiety. Conversely, subtle, rhythmic sounds, preferably natural and harmonious – like the gentle murmur of running water in a small fountain, the delicate tinkling of tuned wind chimes, the distant birdsong at dawn, or soft, relaxing instrumental music – create a sound vibration of tranquility, presence, and connection with the moment.

An energetically healthy home is often one where silence can be heard and appreciated. Not an oppressive or empty silence, but a full, living silence that doesn't bother but welcomes, allowing the mind to quiet and the body to relax. This silence doesn't imply total absence of sound, but the absence of unnecessary noise, of sound pollution assaulting the senses. Creating this more balanced sound environment might mean making conscious decisions like reorganizing appliance use to minimize noise during rest times, better positioning furniture to muffle unwanted echoes in large rooms, using thick rugs or heavy curtains that absorb sound, or introducing positive, healing sounds like a tabletop fountain with circulating water, a radio playing classical or instrumental music at low volume, or simply enjoying the natural sound of wind entering through an open window.

Touch is perhaps the most intimate and direct sense in our relationship with space. It is present in every touch, every contact of skin with the environment. It's in the textures of surfaces surrounding us – walls, furniture, objects. It's in the air temperature felt on the skin. It's in the softness or roughness of fabrics we wrap ourselves in – bedding, towels, sofas, blankets. It's in the sensation underfoot when walking through the house. A house uncomfortable to the touch, dominated by cold materials like polished metal or excess glass, rough surfaces, or plastics and synthetics that don't breathe, tends to repel prolonged stays, true rest, bodily surrender. In stark contrast, surfaces pleasant to the touch, natural fabrics like cotton, linen, or wool, generous and inviting cushions, soft-textured blankets, sun-warmed wood, soft and thick rugs – all these elements invite the body to relax, rest, surrender to the present moment, feel secure and nourished.

Experiencing walking barefoot through the house is a revealing and simple sensory exercise. Perceiving where the floor is cold and unpleasant, where steps make a hollow or sharp noise, and where, conversely, feet feel welcomed, supported. Touching the walls, feeling their texture. Touching furniture, decorative objects. Feeling with hands if there is life, warmth, organicity, or rigidity, coldness, artificiality. Tactile comfort is not a mere superfluous luxury – it's a fundamental biological need communicating to our most primitive nervous system that we are safe, protected, belonging to that place.

Even taste – albeit more indirectly – has its place in the sensory experience of space. The quality of food we prepare and consume, how these foods are organized and presented in the kitchen and on the table, the beauty of chosen tableware, the texture of napkins, the very ritual of setting the table with care and intention before a meal – all significantly contribute to the sense of pleasure, nourishment, and well-being associated with home. A house that feeds the palate with respect, presence, and beauty is a house that also nourishes the soul, celebrates abundance and connection with earth's cycles through food.

Light, in turn, establishes a constant, interactive dialogue with all other senses. It is the great conductor of spatial perception. The quality and intensity of light determine perceived colors, reveal or hide surface textures, define the environment's thermal sensation, and synergistically with sound and aroma, create the complete atmospheres enveloping us. Cold, intense white light in a bedroom, for example, physiologically contradicts any attempt to generate calm and relaxation, even if furniture is extremely comfortable and scents are soft and calming. The body reacts to cold light with an alert state. Conversely, warm, soft yellow light, positioned intentionally via lamps or floor lamps, can transform even a simple corner without many visual attractions into an inviting space for rest, reading, and retreat.

Upon starting to consciously observe the various "senses" of space, how they manifest in each room, one also begins to notice more clearly which areas of the house need more warmth (perhaps more textures, warm colors, yellow light), which ask for more freshness (perhaps more ventilation, plants, light colors, citrus scents), which cry out for silence or, conversely, for a touch of sonic joy. And, from this heightened perception, one can then begin to act more directedly and effectively. Replacing a synthetic fabric with a more pleasant, natural one. Better ventilating a room that seemed stagnant. Adding a small water fountain for the relaxing sound of flow. Planting a lavender pot in the bedroom window. Playing soft music at the beginning or end of the day. Lighting natural incense before sleep or meditation. These are gestures, often small and simple, but when guided by attentive sensory listening, possess the power to transform the entire environment, layer by layer.

This refinement of sensory perception regarding space is also a fascinating path of self-knowledge. Because, by consciously adjusting the sensory stimuli of the surrounding environment, we also inevitably adjust our own internal state. If agitation or anxiety predominates, one instinctively seeks the soft, the gently dark, silence, calming scent. If energy is low or apathy sets in, one seeks fresh citrus scents, clear natural light, the subtle, stimulating sound of the outside world entering through the window. Space begins to function as a sensory mirror of the soul – and the soul, in turn, as a vibrant, sensitive reflection of the space welcoming it.

Cultivating the senses of space is, ultimately, making the house a living, responsive organism, where each room has its specific sensory function and contributes to the whole, each texture has a reason, each scent carries an intention, each sound composes a melody. It's recognizing that deep, lasting well-being resides not just in square footage or object value, but in the quality of presence established with the environment. And that this presence invariably begins with openness and attentive listening through all senses. When all senses are welcomed, respected, and nourished by space, the body relaxes deeply, the mind slows its incessant flow, the heart opens more easily. And home finally becomes a place where it is genuinely good to be – not just because it looks beautiful, but because it is alive, true, in deep resonance with who we are in our most primordial sensory essence.

Chapter 13
Intention and Purpose

The house where we live, like the body we inhabit, can exist merely as a physical, functional structure, a set of walls sheltering us from the elements. Or it can flourish, transcend its materiality, and become a true temple, a sacred space that nourishes the soul and mirrors our inner journey. The fundamental difference between these two realities lies not in the quality of the walls, the luxury of the furniture, or the size of the rooms. It lies, rather, in the meaning imprinted upon these elements, in the consciousness deposited in every corner. A physically empty space can become vibrant and sacred when imbued with a clear, elevated purpose. A common, previously forgotten corner can convert into a welcoming, restorative refuge when charged with loving, conscious intention. Intention and purpose are the invisible yet absolutely essential foundations of a living, coherent, meaningful home aligned with its inhabitant. Without them, the space might fill with things, objects, visual information, but will remain soulless, devoid of that subtle quality that transforms a house into a true home.

Each room in the house possesses, by its nature and location, an inherent energetic vocation, a primary function suggested by Feng Shui or Vastu Shastra principles, or simply by functional logic. The kitchen is naturally a place of nourishment, the bedroom for rest, the living room for socializing. At the same time, each resident carries unique needs, particular desires, specific dreams, and a singular life story. When these two forces – the space's natural vocation and the inhabitant's conscious intention – align harmoniously, the environment begins to vibrate in consonance, reveals its maximum potential, and actively supports those living there in their goals and well-being.

However, when these forces are misaligned, when a space is used contradictorily to its nature or desired intention, energetic confusion sets in. The room begins to be used fragmentedly or inadequately, the flow of energy (Chi) disperses or stagnates, and a subtle yet persistent discomfort starts to settle, often almost imperceptibly at first, but gradually undermining the residents' vitality and clarity.

The practice of imbuing the home with intention begins with a fundamental question, asked for each main room: what purpose does this space serve in my life, right now? And, on a deeper level: what do I truly wish to experience and feel here? What emotion do I want to predominate upon entering this room? What kind of experience do I want this place to offer me and others who share it with me? Discovering the essential purpose of each room is an intimate process of inner listening, of self-knowledge applied to space. It's not about simply applying external rules learned from books or following ready-made interior design formulas. It is, rather, about aligning the space's practical function with its emotional, symbolic, and existential function in your current life.

A bedroom, for example, might be seen merely as a functional place to sleep. But, with intention, it can be transformed into a sanctuary for deep, regenerative rest, a nest of affection and intimacy for a couple, a safe space for dreaming and accessing the unconscious, a silent refuge for retreat and reading. A living room can be merely a place to passively watch television. Or it can be consciously designated as a vibrant family meeting point, a welcoming setting for meaningful conversations and true exchanges, a stage for shared laughter and celebrations, or even a space for comfortable, contemplative silences for two or a group. A kitchen can be just a pragmatic place to quickly prepare food. Or it can become a living laboratory of conscious nutrition, of affective alchemy where love is the main ingredient, of rescuing and celebrating family memory through recipes and aromas.

When the intention for each space becomes clear, defined, and felt in the heart, the physical organization of that space becomes surprisingly simple and intuitive. Everything starts revolving around what is truly essential to sustain that declared purpose. Items not serving this main intention lose their reason for being there and are naturally eliminated or relocated. The choice of decor, lighting, colors, furniture – everything aligns like satellites orbiting the center of meaning established for that environment. And it is precisely this center of clear purpose that sustains the energetic balance and harmony of the place, giving coherence to every choice made.

Establishing a room's intention is like drawing an internal map for the energy one wishes to cultivate there. And each subsequent choice – from the color of a cushion to the position of a painting – becomes a conscious step in that charted direction. If the bedroom's primary purpose is deep rest, then all possible visual (excess objects, vibrant colors) and technological interferences (television, cellphone by the bedside) must be carefully reviewed and ideally eliminated or minimized. If the living room's main intention is conviviality and connection, then the seating arrangement should favor eye-to-eye encounter, circular conversation, not individual alienation before a central screen. If the home office is designated as a space for creation and focus, then it must be organized to inspire, provoke the mind, instigate new ideas – not oppress with piles of paper, disorder, and visual or auditory noise.

This clarity of purpose also allows environments not to accumulate contradictory functions generating energetic conflict. How often do we observe the same room – especially in smaller houses or apartments – simultaneously serving as a bedroom, office, storage for various objects, and even an ironing area? This functional multiplicity might be unavoidable in some limited-space contexts, but if not very well organized and demarcated (physically and energetically), it tends to generate an overlap of conflicting energies and consequent psychic fatigue in residents. Each human activity requires a distinct energetic vibration to be performed fully. Working requires focus (Yang), sleeping requires relaxation (Yin), storing things requires organization (Metal), socializing requires openness (Fire/Wood). When all these activities and their respective energies coexist mixed in the same physical space, without clear division or conscious transition, the mind gets confused, the body becomes exhausted trying to adapt to contradictory stimuli, and the space loses its effectiveness in adequately supporting any of these functions.

Therefore, the act of defining each room's intention can be accompanied and reinforced by small symbolic rituals anchoring this decision in the space's energy field. Writing the main intention for that room on a piece of paper and placing it discreetly in a drawer or under a significant object. Choosing a specific object (a stone, an image, a plant) visually representing this purpose and placing it prominently, yet harmoniously. Creating a small altar, however simple, with elements (candles, crystals, flowers, symbols) constantly reminding of what one wants to live and cultivate there. These gestures, though subtle, hold great power to activate the space as a field of manifestation for that intention. The intention thus takes root not only in the resident's mind but in the very energetic body of the environment.

Coherence between the defined intention and the space's physical organization also greatly facilitates periodic energetic cleansing. Environments without clear, defined purpose tend to become magnets for accumulating random objects, unprocessed feelings, obsolete memories, and stagnant energies from people who passed through. They often transform into deposits of undigested past, into cellars of the soul. Conversely, a space with clear purpose renews itself energetically more continuously and naturally, as it is constantly inhabited with presence and awareness. Every time one enters it, the mind recognizes its meaning, the body responds to its specific vibration, energy circulates more fluidly and directedly. The resident's very intentional presence acts as a constant agent of cleansing and renewal.

The practice of defining spatial intention can also be a powerful tool for strengthening family ties or bonds between housemates. Gathering everyone sharing the home and, together, discussing and deciding the main purpose of each shared room (living room, kitchen, balcony). This dialogue not only helps harmonize the physical space according to everyone's needs but also aligns relationships, promotes mutual understanding and collaboration. When everyone shares the same understanding of a room's function and energy, the use of that space tends to become more respectful, more functional for the group, and consequently, more affective and harmonious.

It's fundamental to understand that this definition of purpose need not – and should not – be rigid or immutable. The house is a living organism because life is dynamic. Needs change, life phases succeed each other, priorities transform. And the intention for each space needs to accompany this dance of existence. A room that was once a nursery can transform into a painting studio when children grow up. An office that was essential might become a guest room upon retirement. A previously forgotten balcony used as storage can become a sacred space for meditation and yoga. What's important is that, with each new configuration, each significant change in the residents' lives, the fundamental question returns: what is the living, essential function of this place for me (or us) *now*?

    This exercise of defining and redefining intentions, though seemingly simple or even obvious, represents a true silent revolution in how we inhabit our spaces. Because the vast majority of houses, unfortunately, are not inhabited with clear intention. They are occupied by inertia, functional necessity, inherited patterns, or those imposed by consumer society. Objects are where they've always been, often without questioning their real utility or meaning. Furniture follows the inherited layout or what seemed most convenient at the time of moving in. Room functions weren't thought out or felt – they were simply imposed by practicality or habit.

    Bringing conscious intention into the home is, therefore, a powerful act of returning to the house its dignity as a sacred extension of being, as a partner in life's journey. When each room of the house has a clear, felt purpose, and each purpose is lived with presence and coherence day by day, the entire house transforms energetically. From a passive, neutral backdrop, it becomes an active collaborator in the residents' well-being, clarity, and fulfillment. From a fragmented, disconnected space, it converts into an integrated, intelligent system, where each part contributes to the harmony of the whole. And each daily gesture – preparing breakfast, making the bed, turning on a light at dusk, sitting down to read – ceases to be a mechanical act to become the material expression of a deeper meaning, a cultivated intention.

The house then begins to truly serve what is essential for the soul. Not empty accumulation. Not superficial appearance. Not constant distraction. What remains after this process of clarity is what sustains. What stays is what truly matters. What vibrates is what has genuine purpose. And in this conscious, aligned vibration, a new, deeper way of dwelling is born: inhabiting not just a physical space defined by walls, but an intentional field of welcome, creation, growth, and spiritual connection. Thus, it matters not the size of the house, nor the monetary value of the furniture filling it. What truly matters is the crystalline clarity of purpose. The luminous sharpness of intention. Because that is what shapes the subtle atmosphere of the home. And it is this atmosphere that, day after day, silently builds and sustains the quality of life one wishes to live.

Chapter 14
Bagua Map

There is a subtle cartography, an invisible map residing in the millennial wisdom of Feng Shui, capable of unveiling the deep connections between the space we inhabit and the diverse areas composing our existence. This tool, silent in its application yet immensely transformative in power, is known as the Bagua Map. It doesn't present itself as a set of inflexible rules or arbitrary impositions on how we should organize our homes. Its nature is more delicate, more reflective. The Bagua functions as a symbolic mirror, a spatial oracle that, when overlaid onto our home's floor plan, reveals how vital energy, Chi, flows – or fails to flow – through sectors corresponding to career, spirituality, family, prosperity, success, relationships, creativity, friends, and health.

The term "Bagua" itself unveils part of its mystery, literally meaning "eight trigrams." These trigrams are ancestral symbols derived from the I Ching, the Book of Changes, one of China's oldest and most revered classic texts. Each trigram consists of a combination of three lines, either continuous (Yang) or broken (Yin), representing the fundamental forces of the universe and their dynamic interactions. The Bagua organizes these eight trigrams around a center, forming an octagonal diagram or, in more modern adaptations for square or rectangular plans, a three-by-three grid, totaling nine energetic sectors or palaces. Each of these sectors, called Guas, pulsates with specific energy, resonating directly with a fundamental aspect of the human journey.

Applying the Bagua over the space we call home is an invitation to an exercise in deep listening, a form of silent dialogue with the house's soul. It's not just about identifying where each Gua is located, but feeling, observing, and understanding how energy manifests in that specific area. The map acts as a guide, pointing out which sectors of the residence are vibrating in harmony with their intrinsic purposes, nourishing the corresponding areas of life, and which may need attention, care, conscious intervention to release blockages or activate dormant potentials.

The house, as explored in previous chapters, functions as a living organism, a sensitive extension of our own being. Every corner, wall, object contained within it resonates, subtly or obviously, with a facet of our experience. The Bagua offers us a language to decipher this resonance.

Imagine, for example, that the area corresponding to Success in your home – that sector governing recognition, reputation, personal brilliance – is located in a dark corner, perhaps a forgotten storage room or a rarely used passageway filled with functionless objects. The Bagua suggests this spatial configuration might symbolically mirror a difficulty in feeling recognized by the world, hesitation in showing your talents, or a sense of invisibility in your professional or personal trajectory. Similarly, if the corner associated with Relationships houses broken objects, remnants of unresolved painful bonds, or simply persistent clutter, even hidden inside closets, harmony in intimate relationships – whether romantic, familial, or friendships – tends to echo this same pattern of imbalance, fragmentation, or difficulty maintaining fluid, healthy connection. Physical space and emotional space dance together, and the Bagua helps us perceive the steps of this invisible choreography.

The practical application of the Bagua, fortunately, doesn't require complex technical knowledge or advanced architectural skills. The starting point is a simple map of the house or apartment. It could be the official floor plan, if available, or even a hand-drawn sketch, as long as it maintains the general proportions of the space. The crucial element for orienting the map, especially in the Feng Shui school known as the Black Hat School (or Tibetan Tantric Buddhism - BTB), very popular in the West, is the main entrance door – the one through which primordial energy, Chi, enters the home. Positioning oneself at the entrance door, looking into the property, the Bagua is mentally (or physically, over the drawing) overlaid onto the space, aligning the map's base (where the Spirituality, Career, and Friends Guas are located) with the wall of the main door. From this reference, the space is divided into the nine energetic sectors.

It's important to note another approach exists, the Compass School (or Classical Feng Shui), which uses actual cardinal directions (North, South, East, West, etc.), determined with a compass, to position the Guas. Both schools are valid and effective, but the Black Hat School is often preferred for its simplicity and adaptability to different construction types, especially in urban environments where cardinal orientation might not be ideal.

Once the Bagua is positioned, each identified sector carries a specific energetic signature, a deep symbolism that can be consciously worked with. We can activate a Gua we wish to strengthen, harmonize one that seems unbalanced, or heal one showing obvious blockages, using colors, shapes, elements, objects, and above all, clear intention.

Let's explore each of these energetic palaces. The Career Gua, also known as Work or Life Path, is located in the central area of the entrance door wall. It represents not only profession but the personal journey, life's flow, the identity we present to the world, and how we move through it. Associated with the Water element and the color black (or very dark shades of blue), this Gua benefits from elements symbolizing fluidity and depth. A rug in dark blue or black tones at the entrance, a well-placed mirror (not directly reflecting the door, to avoid repelling incoming Chi), a small water fountain, or an image evoking movement, like a winding river or the ocean, can positively activate this area. Blockages here, such as an obstructed entrance corridor, a jamming door, a dark or chaotic environment right upon entering, can symbolize difficulties in professional advancement, a sense of stagnation in life, or lack of clarity about one's path. Caring for the entrance is caring for the journey's start.

In the left corner of the entrance (always looking from inside the door towards the interior), we find the Spirituality Gua, also called Wisdom or Knowledge. This sector is intrinsically linked to self-knowledge, inner wisdom, the capacity for study, reflection, and connection with the sacred, whatever that may be for each individual. Its element is Earth (Mountain, in the I Ching) and its associated colors are blue, dark green, and lilac. It's an ideal area for installing libraries, creating a meditation or reading corner, or simply a quiet space for introspection. Books, objects evoking calm (like a mountain image), comfortable cushions, soft lighting, and scents like sandalwood or lavender strengthen this Gua. A chaotic, disorganized environment or one used for storage in this area can reflect mental confusion, difficulty concentrating on studies, lack of spiritual clarity, or a feeling of disconnection from oneself.

Moving to the center of the left wall lies the Family Gua, or Ancestry. This sector governs ties with our roots, relationship with ancestors, the physical and emotional health of the family as a whole, and the structure supporting us. Its element is Wood (Thunder) and its color is vibrant green. It's an excellent place to display happy, well-chosen family photographs (avoiding images of sad moments or people with unresolved conflicts). Healthy, vigorous plants, especially those growing upwards, sturdy wooden furniture, and objects symbolizing growth and family unity positively activate this energy. The presence of broken furniture, damaged objects, painful memories associated with family conflicts, or disorder in this sector can indicate imbalances in family bonds, recurring health problems, or a feeling of lack of support and structure.

In the back left corner, farthest from the door on the left wall, we find one of the most celebrated Guas: Prosperity, also known as Wealth or Abundance. Here symbolically resides the flow of material abundance, but also prosperity in all senses – health, relationships, opportunities, generosity, and the feeling of deservingness. Its element is also Wood (Wind) and its colors are purple, lilac, and gold. To enhance this area, we can use healthy, leafy plants (like Zamioculcas or the Money Tree), a small water fountain with gentle, constant flow (moving water symbolizes financial flow), golden objects or those evoking wealth (like Chinese coins, crystals such as citrine or pyrite), or a personal symbol of abundance. It's crucial this area is always clean, organized, and clutter-free. Accumulating forgotten, broken objects, trash, or neglecting this area can reflect blockages in financial flow, difficulties in receiving, or a limiting belief about one's own worthiness and ability to generate wealth.

At the center of the back wall, opposite the entrance door, is the Success Gua, also called Fame or Recognition. This sector relates to our reputation, how we are seen by the world, our personal brilliance, public image, and the ability to achieve our goals and be recognized for them. The associated element is Fire and the predominant color is vibrant red (orange, bright yellow, or gold can also be used). To activate this area, we can use objects symbolizing personal achievements (diplomas, trophies, photos of successful moments), strong, well-positioned lighting (like a directed spotlight), objects in triangular or pyramid shapes, or a piece of art with warm, vibrant colors representing passion and recognition. A dark, abandoned, excessively neutral environment, or one with objects reminding of failures or frustrations in this area, may indicate difficulty standing out, fear of exposure, reputation problems, or a feeling of not being seen or valued for one's efforts.

In the back right corner, farthest from the door on the right wall, we find the Relationships Gua. This sector deeply resonates with affective bonds, especially romantic relationships, but also covers partnerships, societies, and the relationship with the inner feminine (anima). Its element is Earth (Receptive Earth) and its colors are pink, white, and soft pastels. The energy of this Gua is strengthened by duality and balance. It's ideal to keep objects in pairs: two identical lamps, two candles, two identical cushions, a pair of mandarin ducks (traditional symbol of union), or images evoking love, affection, and partnership. Photos of the couple (if any) in happy moments are welcome. It's important to avoid solitary objects, sad images or those reminding of separations, or the presence of items related to work or people other than the partner. A disorganized, forgotten corner with broken objects or symbols of loneliness in this area may reflect relationship difficulties, loneliness, imbalance in love life, or problems in partnerships.

The center of the Bagua, the heart of the house, is the Health Gua, also known as Tai Chi. This point is crucial, influencing and balancing all other Guas. It represents physical, mental, and spiritual health, overall balance, and the vitality of the home and its residents. Its element is Earth and its color is yellow (or earthy, ochre tones). The fundamental recommendation for this area is to keep it as free, clean, and well-lit as possible. Avoid heavy furniture, partitions, stairs, or bathrooms located exactly in the center of the house. If there are obstructions, the vital energy of the entire space can be compromised, generating feelings of heaviness, difficulty making decisions, health problems, or general imbalance. To strengthen the center, use square rugs in yellow or earth tones, ceramic objects, crystals like clear or yellow quartz, and keep the area always organized with good air and light circulation. The center is the point of union, the axis supporting the wheel of life reflected in the home.

Moving to the center of the right wall, we find the Creativity Gua, also associated with Children (whether literal children or projects and ideas "born" from us). This sector is linked to creative expression in all its forms, joy, pleasure, spontaneity, fertility (symbolic or literal), and the relationship with childhood (ours and our children's). Its element is Metal (Lake) and its color is white (or metallic pastels, like silver). It's an excellent location for an art corner, with painting, drawing, or writing materials, musical instruments, toys (if there are children), or playful, colorful objects evoking joy and expression. Paintings with vibrant abstract art, sculptures with rounded shapes, or polished metal objects also activate this energy. A sterile, gloomy, disorganized, or neglected space here can indicate creative blocks, difficulty expressing one's truth, problems in relationships with children, or lack of joy and pleasure in life.

Finally, in the bottom right corner, near the entrance door on the right wall, lies the Friends Gua, also called Helpful People, Benefactors, or Travel. This sector governs social connections, supportive friends, guiding mentors, unexpected help received from the universe, and also travel (physical or spiritual) expanding our horizons. Its element is Metal (Heaven) and its colors are gray, white, and black. To activate this area, we can use photographs of dear friends in happy moments, images of places we wish to visit or that inspire us, globes, maps, metal objects (like bells or sculptures), or symbols representing protection and spiritual support (like angels or guides). Keeping this area organized, perhaps with a place to store business cards or important contacts, also strengthens the support network. Disorder, broken objects, or the absence of elements symbolizing connection in this Gua can reflect social isolation, lack of support, or difficulties in traveling and expanding horizons.

With this symbolic map overlaid on the house plan, the resident is invited to look at their space with new depth. Each corner ceases to be just functional square footage and gains broader meaning, existential resonance. A simple furniture rearrangement, painting a wall, placing a plant, or removing an object no longer vibrating in harmony cease to be random acts and transform into gestures charged with intention, conscious dialogues with one's own energy field. Removing an accumulated object from a specific Gua can symbolically mean releasing energy trapped in that corresponding life area. Placing an inspiring image, a crystal, or a specific color can be a conscious call to nourish a forgotten aspect of oneself, to invite a new frequency to manifest.

However, it's fundamental to reiterate that the Bagua is not a magic formula, nor a set of dogmatic rules. It is an invitation to exploration, a tool for spatial self-knowledge. Intuition plays a crucial role in this process. If the suggested area for a certain Gua doesn't exactly match the room's current use (e.g., the Prosperity Gua falls on a bathroom), there's no need to panic. Feng Shui offers cures and adjustments to harmonize these situations. We can use colors, mirrors, crystals, or specific elements to neutralize unfavorable energies or enhance desired ones, adapting the symbology to the reality of the space. Sensitive listening to the particular language of that house, that apartment, is always paramount.

What truly matters is that meaning reveals itself through interaction with the map, that the connection between space and life becomes conscious, and that the house gradually transforms into an increasingly authentic and potent reflection of an intentionally lived existence.

With time and practice, the resident begins to perceive the subtle signs of this interaction. Small changes made in the environment, focusing on a specific Gua, start resonating in internal changes, emotional unblocking, mental clarity, unexpected synchronicities arising in the corresponding life area. The home thus transforms into a symbolic chessboard of personal growth, an alchemical laboratory where matter and spirit dance together. And the Bagua reveals itself as a precious compass – not to dictate rigid paths, but to illuminate the journey, constantly reminding us that the physical space we tread is intrinsically intertwined with the paths we choose to walk in life. Every corner of the home, from this perspective, dialogues with the soul. And when the soul is willing to listen, when consciousness opens to this dance between the visible and the invisible, everything begins to align – inside and out, matter and energy. The Bagua Map, in this broad and deep context, transcends a mere spatial organization tool. It becomes a means of returning to the house its sacred, symbolic, transformative dimension. And, simultaneously, returns to the resident the power to walk through their own life with more awareness, clarity, presence, and harmony.

Chapter 15
Light and Color

In the silent theater that is our home, two actors play absolute leading roles, although their performances often go unnoticed by the hurried consciousness of daily life. They are light and color. Together, they not only define an environment's aesthetics and atmosphere but act as subtle conductors of our emotional, physical, and even spiritual vibration. They paint the air we breathe, shape the perception of space, and directly interfere with the quality of our vital energy. A house bathed in appropriate light, respecting natural cycles, and dressed in colors vibrating in harmony with its purposes and the soul of its inhabitant, resembles a pulsating living organism, attuned to the resident's internal time and the essential frequency of life itself. Understanding the depth and power of these two silent forces – the revealing light and the expressive color – is opening the door to redesign not only the space's appearance but its very energetic essence, transforming the home into a true field of healing and well-being.

Light, in its purest, most primordial manifestation, is the golden bridge connecting the outer universe to our inner refuge. Sunlight, in particular, transcends the mere function of illuminating; it is an active agent of healing, balance, and vitality. Our body responds to it intrinsically and profoundly. Circadian rhythms, governing our sleep-wake cycles, are directly regulated by exposure to natural light. Our mood, concentration ability, sleep quality, and even appetite are influenced by the presence – or absence – of sun rays in our daily lives. A house generously welcoming sunlight, allowing it to dance through rooms throughout the day, is a house breathing vitality. And a home that breathes inevitably becomes an environment conducive to healing, well-being, and mental clarity.

For this reason, the first step in harmonizing a space through light involves attentive, sensitive observation of its natural path. Are windows obstructed by heavy furniture, opaque curtains blocking brightness, or bars creating unwanted shadows? Are eaves excessively long, preventing sun entry, especially in winter months? Could mirrors be strategically positioned to capture light from a window and reflect it into darker corners, expanding luminosity and the sense of spaciousness? A single well-thought-out reflection can operate a remarkable transformation in a room's atmosphere. Choosing a lighter, translucent fabric for curtains can allow light passage, creating a soft, poetic filter without compromising necessary privacy. And the simple yet powerful act of opening windows daily, allowing air exchange and direct light entry, functions as a daily ritual of energetic renewal, an invitation for fresh, vibrant Chi to nourish the environment.

However, the dance of light doesn't end at sunset. Artificial lighting takes the stage during the night or in environments that, due to their architecture, receive little natural sunlight. The careful choice of this lighting is decisive for atmosphere and well-being. Cold, white lights (with high color temperature, measured in Kelvin), often used by default in many homes and offices, are frequently incompatible with the feeling of welcome and relaxation we seek at home. They tend to stimulate the mind, accelerate the internal rhythm, and create a sense of distance, being more suitable for work environments requiring maximum alertness. Conversely, warm lights – with yellowish or orange hues (low color temperature) – evoke feelings of shelter, comfort, intimacy, and repose. They mimic the light of a fireplace or candles, connecting us to an ancestral memory of safety and warmth.

The same room can gain multiple personalities and functionalities through the intelligent use of different light points and types. General lighting, perhaps on the ceiling, can serve more practical activities. Lamps with shades diffusing light create cozy niches for reading or intimate conversations. Candles, used safely and intentionally, offer a living, dancing light, perfect for moments of introspection, meditation, or romance. Light intensity is also crucial; using dimmers allows adjusting luminosity according to need and time of day, creating flexibility that accompanies internal rhythms. Artificial light, therefore, is not just a substitute for sunlight; it is a moldable tool, capable of sculpting atmospheres and simultaneously modulating our state of mind, emotions, and physical disposition.

If light is the revealer, color is the visible expression of energy itself. Each hue, shade, saturation carries a unique vibrational frequency. This frequency interacts directly with our energy centers, nervous system, and psyche, even if we're not fully conscious of this interaction. Colors are not mere decorative elements applied to surfaces; they are a powerful language, a form of non-verbal communication evoking emotions, awakening sensations, and influencing our breathing and mood. When choosing colors to dress an environment, we are actually choosing the type of energy we wish it to emanate, the quality of vibration we want to cultivate in that space.

Each room, with its specific function within the home's dynamic, calls for a particular emotional tone, a palette supporting its purpose. Blue tones, for example, in their various variations from soft sky-blue to deep indigo, are known for their calming and tranquilizing qualities. They invite inner silence, introspection, mental serenity. They are ideal for bedrooms, favoring restorative sleep, for meditation or study spaces, aiding concentration, or for bathrooms, evoking water's purity and fluidity. Greens, connecting us directly to nature, bring feelings of freshness, balance, healing, and stability. Moss green grounds, leaf green revitalizes, seafoam green refreshes. They work very well in living rooms, kitchens (symbolizing health and vitality), offices (promoting calm focus), or any space where the Wood element's regenerative energy is desired.

Yellow, the sun's color, in variations from pale to vibrant, activates the mind, stimulates communication, joy, optimism, and intellectual focus. It's an excellent color for social areas, dining rooms (where it can stimulate appetite and conversation), kitchens, creative offices, or children's rooms, but should be used balancedly to avoid agitation. Orange tones, warm and welcoming, inherit yellow's energy and red's intensity. They bring people closer, favor affective communication, enthusiasm, and a sense of comfort. They can be very welcome in dining rooms, social areas, kitchens, or hallways, creating an inviting, warm atmosphere.

Red, in turn, is the color of primordial vital energy, passion, action, power. It's the Fire element's color in its maximum expression. Being very stimulating, it should be used moderately and intentionally, preferably in strategic points – an accent wall, cushions, decorative objects. In excess, red can cause agitation, irritability, or anxiety. It's a powerful color for activating areas linked to success or passion but requires caution. Pink, especially in softer, delicate versions, is the color of tenderness, affective connection, unconditional love, and self-care. It's ideal for master bedrooms, children's rooms, or any space where cultivating an atmosphere of kindness, compassion, and receptivity is desired.

Neutral tones – like beige, off-white variations, light gray, sand color – offer a base of stability, calm, and elegance. They visually expand spaces and serve as a canvas for other elements to stand out. However, if used excessively without counterpoints of texture or warmth, they can make the environment cold or monotonous. The secret lies in combining them with natural materials, warm lighting, and subtle color points. Earthy tones – browns, ochres, terracotta – connect us with Earth's strength, ancestry, security, and grounding. They can be incorporated through floors, wood furniture, rustic fabrics like linen or jute, or ceramic and clay objects. Darker tones, like graphite, navy blue, petrol green, or burgundy, bring depth, mystery, sophistication, and an invitation to introspection. They should be used sparingly, usually on accent walls, specific furniture, or details, and always balanced with lighter elements and good lighting, so the environment doesn't become heavy or oppressive.

Applying these colors can happen in innumerable ways. It's not limited to painting walls. Fabrics for curtains, sofas, cushions, and rugs; furniture with colored finishes; decorative objects like vases, paintings, sculptures; even the color of tableware or kitchen utensils – everything contributes to the environment's chromatic palette. Often, it's not necessary to paint an entire room to renew its energy. A single wall with a well-chosen accent color, or introducing new cushions and a vibrant rug, can already significantly alter the space's vibrational field. Experimentation is welcome, always guided by the feeling one seeks to create.

It's also important to consider the house's overall chromatic harmony, the flow of colors between different rooms. Some homes have completely distinct, disconnected palettes in each room, which can create a sense of visual and energetic fragmentation. Others feature excessive homogeneity of neutral tones, resulting in visual boredom or lack of vitality. The ideal is to seek balance: each space can have its chromatic identity, aligned with its function, but there should be a connecting thread – perhaps a base color palette repeated in details, or aesthetic coherence in materials and finishes – uniting the whole, creating a sense of unity and harmonious flow throughout the house.

Colors can also be chosen intentionally to activate specific life areas, according to the Bagua Map. The Prosperity corner, for example, benefits from shades of purple, emerald green, or gold. The Relationships sector is favored by shades of pink, soft red, or earthy colors in pairs. The Career area resonates with black or dark blue. Again, this doesn't necessarily mean painting walls these colors, but introducing them symbolically and balancedly through objects, fabrics, artworks, or visual details carrying that intention.

It's fundamental to recognize our relationship with colors is dynamic. A tone that once inspired us and brought comfort might, over time, start to bother or seem inappropriate. A color that brought vitality at one moment might become tiring or excessive in another phase of life. This is perfectly natural, as we change, our internal cycles alter, and the house, as a sensitive mirror, needs to accompany this mutation. Color is also a reflection of our internal state. Changing a wall color, swapping cushion covers, or introducing a new painting can be a powerful gesture to mark the beginning of a new phase, to allow new energy to flourish with more truth and alignment.

Finally, the master key to a truly living, harmonious environment lies in the exquisite balance between light and color. A wisely chosen color, applied under inadequate lighting, loses much of its expressive and vibrational potential. Beautiful, well-designed light, shining on a soulless wall or one with an energy-draining color, cannot transform the atmosphere alone. But when light and color dialogue in harmony, when they dance together in tune with the room's intention and the inhabitant's sensitivity, the space gains soul, depth, presence. It becomes more than a set of surfaces and volumes; it transforms into a vibrational field that nourishes and inspires.

Light and color are the invisible language of the home's soul. They speak directly to our unconscious, bypassing the barriers of the rational mind. And therefore, when well-chosen, when in balance, no one needs to explain why they feel good in that place – the body feels it, the heart recognizes it, the mind quiets. The house then becomes a chromatic and luminous field of healing, authentic expression, and profound harmony. By understanding that every ray of light entering the window and every centimeter of color dressing our walls are integral parts of a living, interconnected organism, we discover that transforming space is, in essence, transforming the very frequency of our lives. And living in harmony with light and color is, ultimately, living in full tune with our own luminous essence.

Chapter 16
Natural Materials

In an era marked by speed, artificiality, and surfaces that mimic but rarely embody the essence of what they represent, a deep yearning for reconnection emerges. We seek, often unknowingly, the touch of truth, the texture that tells stories, the matter that breathes alongside us. The touch of living wood under fingers, the smell of raw earth after rain, the irregular, unique shine of hand-molded ceramics – there is a silent wisdom, an ancestral resonance in natural materials that no synthetic compound, however technologically advanced, can truly imitate. Amidst a daily life often plasticized, automated, where textures tend towards flat uniformity and surfaces shine with excessive, cold polish, the presence of nature inside the home, manifested through the materials we choose to surround ourselves with, becomes a powerful antidote. It's a return to the essential, a reclaiming of our intrinsic connection with the organic world, a way to reconnect with what pulses beneath our feet, in oceans, in forests, sustaining us with its density, imperfect beauty, and profound vitality.

Choosing natural materials to compose our home environment transcends mere aesthetic or decorative decision; it is, fundamentally, a vibrational choice. Each element from nature – whether wood, stone, fiber, clay, or metal in its rawest state – carries a geological or biological history, a unique energetic signature, an intrinsic quality communicating life, time, and transformation. Unlike industrialized materials, often seeking standardization, immutability, and tending towards a certain energetic silence, materials coming directly from the earth, plants, or animals breathe with the environment. They age, acquire patina, change color with light exposure, react to air humidity, absorb and release subtle scents, dynamically interact with the space and its inhabitant. And this discreet vitality, this capacity to be in constant dialogue with the surroundings, reverberates positively in body, mind, and spirit, nurturing a sense of well-being, belonging, and balance.

Modern science itself, through the concept of Biophilia – our innate affinity for all living things – begins to prove what ancestral traditions always knew: surrounding oneself with nature, even in fragments, is essential for human health.

Wood, for example, is much more than a visual resource conferring coziness and warmth to environments. Each piece of wood is a record of time, carrying in its fibers the memory of forests it came from, the history of growth cycles, the seasons it weathered. Solid wood furniture, especially when treated with natural oils or waxes instead of synthetic varnishes sealing its pores, continues interacting with the environment: releasing subtle scents, reacting to air humidity by expanding or contracting slightly, warming welcomingly to the touch. It lives with the house, aging with dignity. A natural wood floor, besides being beautiful, warms the feet, absorbs noise creating more pleasant acoustics, and offers a solid base connected to the earth. Exposed wooden planks on the ceiling, or apparent beams, create not only a rustic or elegant aesthetic effect but also evoke an ancestral feeling of shelter, protective structure. There are countless wood varieties, each with its color, texture, density – from light, soft pine to robust, dark oak, flexible, sustainable bamboo to reclaimed woods loaded with history – offering a vast range of expressive and energetic possibilities.

Natural fibers – like organic cotton, rustic linen, cozy wool, luminous silk, resistant hemp, or earthy textured sisal and jute – bring a tactile, breathable quality to the environment inviting comfort and sensuality. Fabrics of plant or animal origin, especially when not subjected to aggressive chemical treatments or heavy synthetic dyes, allow skin to breathe, help regulate body temperature, and make the experience of dwelling more sensitive, more connected to natural cycles. A raw linen curtain moving gently with the breeze brings lightness and poetry to the space. A sisal or jute rug, with its firm, natural texture, connects feet directly to the ground, offering a sense of grounding and stability. A pure wool blanket, with its variations in texture and incomparable warmth, warms body and soul with ancestral dignity, recalling early human shelters. Cotton, in sheets or upholstery, offers softness and coolness. Each fiber has its own tactile and visual language.

Stone, in turn, offers the home the energy of stability, lasting presence, Earth's silent strength. Surfaces of granite, marble, slate, quartzite, or even less conventional stones like volcanic basalt, porous sandstone, or river pebbles, have the power to anchor the space's energy, create points of density and solidity balancing the fluidity of other elements. Used in kitchen countertops, high-traffic area floors, bathroom claddings, fireplaces, or even decorative details like sculptures, vases, or simply natural stones arranged, natural stone introduces a quality of permanence and resistance. Its coolness to the touch is physical, but its energetic vibration is often warm and protective, coming from deep within the earth, carrying the memory of millions of years of geological formation.

Ceramics, baked clay, exposed brick – materials born from moist earth, shaped by human hands, transformed by fire – bring the beauty of artisanal imperfection indoors. Their surfaces are often unique, with small irregularities, color variations, grooves, organic curves, pores that breathe. Used in plant pots, everyday tableware, rustic floors, hand-painted tiles, or wall coverings, these materials convey authenticity, human warmth, a direct link to manual culture and the singular touch of their creator. They are materials celebrating uniqueness, welcoming the mark of time and use, and thus, bring a layer of truth and soul to the space, aligning perfectly with the Wabi-Sabi philosophy finding beauty in imperfection and transience.

Bamboo, a fast-growing grass of great resistance, is another notable example of natural material carrying multiple energetic qualities: representing accelerated growth, flexibility, resilience, and sustainability. Used in floors, furniture, mats, blinds, room dividers, or decorative objects, bamboo brings a unique combination of visual lightness and structural firmness to the space, associated with the Wood element's expansion energy. Straw, dried leaves woven into baskets, lampshades, or panels, wicker or rattan objects – all these elements rescue the artisan's ancestral gesture and return the beauty of functional simplicity to the home, the connection with manual work and nature's cycles.

The conscious choice for natural materials also implies direct care for residents' health. Environments saturated with plastics, synthetic resins, formaldehyde glues, aggressive varnishes, paints with high levels of volatile organic compounds (VOCs), and other chemical products continuously release toxic particles and gases into indoor air. This invisible pollution can affect the quality of air we breathe, contributing to respiratory problems, allergies, headaches, and other long-term health imbalances. Conversely, a house prioritizing solid wood furniture treated with natural products, organic fabrics without toxic dyes, ecological water-based or lime paints, and other materials that "breathe" and don't emit harmful substances, significantly reduces the invisible toxic load. Thus, a healthier space is created, conducive to restorative rest, physical vitality, and hormonal balance.

Recent scientific studies reinforce this intuitive perception about natural materials' benefits. Research in environmental psychology and neuroarchitecture demonstrates that the mere presence of wood in closed environments can reduce blood pressure, decrease heart rate, and lower levels of cortisol, the stress hormone. Natural textures, like those found in stones, fibers, or raw woods, stimulate the parasympathetic nervous system, responsible for relaxation responses, calm, and feelings of safety. It's as if the human body, upon physical contact with nature's elements, recognizes a familiar, safe environment, activating a deep cellular memory of belonging and well-being. This biophilic connection brings peace and balance almost instantly.

Incorporating natural materials at home doesn't necessarily mean transforming the house into a rustic cabin or adopting a specific style. Integration can occur gradually, subtly, adapted to personal style and functional needs. Replacing a plastic chair with a wooden or bamboo one. Swapping synthetic cushion covers for linen, cotton, or wool. Including a handmade ceramic vase instead of an industrialized glass one. Using natural fiber curtains filtering light softly. Opting for a stone or wood countertop in the kitchen instead of artificial laminates. Using straw baskets for organization. Choosing a jute or sisal rug to define a space. Small gestures that, added together, gradually rebuild the space's sensory and energetic atmosphere, making it more alive and breathable.

This choice for natural materials also often aligns with a stance of greater respect and awareness towards the planet. Natural materials, especially from sustainable sources (like certified woods or bamboo), local production, and which are durable or biodegradable, reduce the environmental impact associated with extracting, producing, and disposing of synthetic petroleum-derived materials. Valuing craftsmanship, fair production chains, and materials that can return to the earth without causing pollution is part of a virtuous cycle of respect: from nature to home, and from home back to nature.

And finally, there is an invisible yet invaluable worth in using these materials: the beauty of patina, the presence of time. Natural materials age. And, unlike synthetics that degrade or lose shine, many natural materials become even more beautiful with passing years and marks of use. A wooden tabletop gently darkening where hands frequently rest. A stone floor gaining natural polish in high-traffic areas. A linen fabric becoming softer with each wash. Leather acquiring marks and nuances telling the story of its user. Time inscribes its unique calligraphy on these materials, humanizing them, singling them out, bringing them affectively closer to the resident. A relationship of memory, shared history, coexistence is created. Synthetic surfaces, designed to look perpetually new or be quickly discarded, rarely commit to the house's soul in this way. Natural materials, however, wear marks of use like medals of honor, silent witnesses to the life that happened there.

By surrounding ourselves with these authentic, living elements, the house transforms into a sensitive, interactive ecosystem. Wood dialogues with light and humidity. Stone responds to ambient temperature. Fabric filters sound and light. Clay breathes. The body feels this organicity, recognizes nature's language, and relaxes. Space ceases to be an inert setting and becomes extended body, expanded skin, embodied nature. And living there is living closer to oneself, more connected to Earth, more immersed in one's own life. Because, after all, nature never left us; we are the ones who sometimes distance ourselves from it. Bringing its materials back indoors is an act of rescue, a silent reminder of what we were, what we are, and what we can still be in our purest essence. A simple gesture in form, but profoundly transformative in vibration. A silent reclaiming of the forgotten harmony between human beings and the natural world.

Chapter 17
Living Elements

There is a silent pulsation, an energy manifesting subtly but unmistakably, when life is invited to enter and settle within our home. It's not enough just to arrange objects meticulously, distribute furniture with geometric balance, choose harmonious colors pleasing to the eye, or apply symbolic maps guiding energy. The house, to become truly habitable in its fullness, to vibrate with a force transcending inanimate matter, needs life. Life expressed in the form of plants that grow and transform, water flowing in constant motion, the flame dancing in a candle, air circulating freely, and the natural presence that breathes, interacts, and marks time's rhythm within the built space. Living elements should not be seen merely as decorative ornaments added to the domestic scene; they are vibrant presences, active participants in the home's energetic ecology, capable of transforming the atmosphere, nourishing the subtle field, and returning the house's original breath of nature, reconnecting it to existence's incessant flow.

Plants, undoubtedly, figure among the most powerful and beneficial silent inhabitants a house can welcome. Their strength lies not only in the aesthetic beauty of their leaves and flowers or the visual freshness they provide, but primarily in their extraordinary ability to transmute environments' energy. Plants breathe with us, in a constant exchange of gases sustaining us mutually. They filter the air, absorbing toxins and releasing pure oxygen. They naturally humidify the environment, making it more comfortable, especially in dry climates or spaces with air conditioning. They renew Chi, vital energy, absorbing stagnations and spreading vitality through their stems, sprouts, leaves, and roots connecting to the earth, even if contained in a pot. The mere presence of a living, healthy, well-cared-for plant, in any room of the house, functions as an eloquent affirmation that this space maintains an active, respectful relationship with the natural world. It's a verdant reminder that the house doesn't need to be an isolated shelter against nature, but can be, and ideally is, an extension of it, a microcosm where life flourishes.

Choosing plant species to introduce into the home should be done sensitively, respecting both the environment's conditions (light, ventilation, humidity) and the rhythm and care availability of those living there. Some plants demand direct sun to thrive, while others prefer diffused light or even partial shade. Some require frequent watering and constantly moist soil, whereas others, like succulents and cacti, are adapted to drier conditions and survive with very little water. The secret to harmonious coexistence lies not in randomly filling the house with pots following trends, but in creating real bonds with chosen species. It means dedicating time to know their names, observe their responses to light and temperature changes, intuitively feel when they need water or nutrients, celebrate a new leaf's birth as a small daily miracle.

Species like succulents and cacti are ideal for sunny windowsills or very bright balconies, requiring little watering and maintenance. Plants like Snake Plant (Sansevieria trifasciata), Pothos (Epipremnum aureum), and ZZ Plant (Zamioculcas zamiifolia) are known for their resilience and adaptability to places with indirect light or even low luminosity, besides being considered excellent air purifiers and energetic protectors in Feng Shui. Ferns, with their delicate, arching foliage, appreciate humidity and shade, being great options for well-ventilated bathrooms or shadier corners of the house. Plants with larger, more exuberant leaves, like the Swiss Cheese Plant (Monstera deliciosa), various types of Philodendrons, Peace Lily (Spathiphyllum wallisii), or small indoor palms (like Lady Palm or Areca Palm), bring volume, texture, and an almost sculptural presence to environments, ideal for living rooms, entry halls, or wide corridors, where they can become focal points of vitality. Trailing plants, like ivies, bridal veil, or pothos itself, can soften right angles of shelves or bookcases, fill empty corners with a cascade of green, or create natural frames for windows and doors. Pots with aromatic herbs – basil, rosemary, mint, sage, thyme, oregano, lavender – can inhabit the kitchen, balcony, or a sunny windowsill, bringing not only green freshness but also delicious aroma and a direct link to food, transforming cooking into a ritual even more connected to the earth.

However, it's crucial to remember a plant's energy is directly linked to its health and the care it receives. A dead, sick, dusty, or visibly neglected plant emits a vibration opposite to what's sought when introducing life into the environment. It becomes a symbol of stagnation, carelessness, vital energy draining away. It's preferable to have a single radiant, well-cared-for plant receiving attention and affection, than many languishing in corners, forgotten and lifeless. Life, when invited to participate in our intimate space, demands exchange, a reciprocal relationship. And this exchange, this dedicated care, is itself a pact of presence, a mindfulness exercise connecting us to the natural rhythm of growth and transformation.

Another living element of great energetic potency, often associated with prosperity and flow in Feng Shui, is moving water. Water is the universal symbol of emotion, intuition, cleansing, adaptability, and flowing abundance. Stagnant water can generate stagnation (Sha Chi), but gently flowing water activates and renews Chi, inviting life's continuous movement, emotional renewal, and prosperity circulation. Small tabletop fountains with a delicate sound of running water, ornamental ponds in gardens, well-kept aquariums, or even simple containers with fresh, clean water renewed regularly, are effective ways to bring water's dynamic, purifying energy indoors. The soft sound of moving water has a proven calming effect on the nervous system, helping reduce stress, stabilize emotions, and refresh the environment's atmosphere.

However, it's important the sound is pleasant, constant, and not excessively loud or intermittent. Noisy fountains, poorly positioned ones (e.g., in bedrooms, disturbing sleep, or directing flow out of the house), or those with dirty, stagnant water produce the opposite effect: generating anxiety, mental noise, feelings of blockage, or energy loss. Water, to be beneficial, needs to be clean, clear, and in harmonious motion.

A well-kept aquarium, with healthy fish and a balanced environment, can also function as a powerful Chi activator and visual anchor for contemplation. The graceful movements of fish, the subtle ballet of aquatic plants, light reflecting on the liquid surface create a relaxing, meditative micro-atmosphere. However, it's fundamental to remember an aquarium demands responsibility and constant care. Fish and other aquatic beings are not mere decorative objects; they are lives entirely dependent on our attention, zeal, respect. A dirty aquarium, with murky water or sick fish, becomes a source of negative energy.

Even if having fountains or aquariums isn't possible, there are symbolic, effective ways to include living water energy in the space: a transparent glass jar with fresh water and some green leaves or flowers, renewed daily; a ceramic bowl with water and floating flower petals; or simply keeping plant vase water always clean and fresh. The very gesture of filling a container with clean water and placing it intentionally in a specific spot already activates the archetype of flow, purification, receptivity.

Besides plants and water, other living elements, though less obvious, significantly contribute to home vitality. Natural light entering the window and warming a surface, creating a dynamic play of light and shadow throughout the day. Wind crossing an open window, bringing sounds and scents from the outside world and gently moving curtains or mobiles. The smell of moist earth after watering plants. The living, dancing flame of a candle lit with intention, representing the Fire element in its purest, most transformative form. All this is living nature in constant dialogue with the house. They are not static objects, but manifestations of life in motion, altering the space's sensory and energetic perception.

And, of course, there are the living beings actively sharing space with us: pets. A dog wagging its tail upon greeting us, bringing joy and movement. A cat purring on a lap, offering calm and presence. A bird singing at dawn, greeting the new day with melody. They should not be seen as mere instruments to activate Feng Shui energy, but as family members, sentient beings with soul, free will, particular rhythms. They predominantly bring Yang energy – active, dynamic, sociable, transformative – to the home. They demand presence, care, responsibility, attentive listening to their needs. In return, they offer unconditional love, companionship, and teach us about loyalty, simplicity, the joy of living in the present moment. Interaction with pets is proven to reduce stress and improve emotional well-being.

Even for those who, for various reasons, cannot have animals, living plants, or fountains at home, it's still possible to create a space resonating with life's energy. Opening oneself to the presence of nature already existing around is the first step. Consciously observing how sunlight moves through the environment throughout the day. Feeling the sun's warmth on the skin for a few minutes near the window. Perceiving the smell of wind after rain. Bringing indoors small treasures found in nature during a walk: an interestingly shaped dry branch, a smooth stone found on the beach, a perfect shell, a dry leaf with vibrant autumn colors. Nature is everywhere, in its most diverse forms – one just needs to develop the sensitivity to listen to and welcome it.

When these living elements – whether plants, water, fire, air, animals, or nature symbols – are consciously integrated into the home, something fundamental changes in its atmosphere. The air seems lighter, fresher. Time seems to slow down, inviting calm. The body relaxes more easily. The mind finds more silence. The soul smiles in recognition. Because life recognizes and responds to life. And when the house is alive, pulsating, connected to natural cycles, it ceases to be just a physical, functional shelter. It becomes fertile ground for personal growth, a nest that welcomes and protects, a seedbed of possibilities where new ideas, emotions, experiences can germinate.

Surrounding oneself with living elements is, in essence, an act of remembering one's own vitality. It's recognizing that we too grow, breathe, transform in constant cycles. It's dissolving the rigidity of built form and allowing nature – the one dwelling within us and around us – to find welcoming, expressive lodging within what we call home.

Chapter 18
Sound and Scent

In a home that breathes harmony, the experience transcends what the eyes can capture. While light dances on surfaces, revealing shapes and colors, and objects occupy their places in the space's choreography, there exist even subtler, almost ethereal layers that vibrate and move far beyond vision's reach. They hover in the air like invisible presences, penetrate the skin without asking permission, pass through our senses in deep silence or soft melody, in delicate fragrance or powerful olfactory memory. These layers are woven by sound and scent, two intangible travelers acting as true alchemists of the domestic environment. They possess the unique ability to transform the atmosphere without physically touching anything, exerting a mysterious, profound power: that of altering a space's soul, its inhabitants' mood, and the quality of vital energy, often without us consciously perceiving where the change originated or what the transforming agent was.

Let's begin our exploration with the universe of sounds, which echo not only through the house's walls and structures but resonate directly in the internal states of each person living there. Some houses seem to whisper calm and tranquility, where silence is filled with soft, natural sounds. Others seem to scream tension, immersed in constant, dissonant noises. Some vibrate with the harmonious tinkling of strategically placed wind chimes, while others are muffled by thick, repetitive, monotonous noises – the hum of appliances, traffic noise, the incessant sound of the television – which, being so constant, become almost imperceptible to consciousness but continue affecting the nervous system. Feng Shui, in its holistic approach, does not ignore this sound field; on the contrary, it recognizes in it a powerful current of moving energy, capable of elevating and harmonizing Chi (vital energy) or contaminating and stagnating it, according to its nature and intensity.

Pleasant, harmonious, natural sounds function as openers of invisible paths; they dissolve energetic rigidities accumulated in the air, break stagnation patterns, and restore the environment's vibrational balance, acting like a fresh breeze blowing over still waters, bringing movement and clarity.

To consciously work with sound, the first step is developing attentive listening to the house. Try closing your eyes in different rooms and at different times of day, focusing only on present sounds. Where do tensions resonate? Where does silence seem dense and heavy? Where are there aggressive or irritating noises normalized by routine? The persistent hum of an electric transformer outside, the constant noise of vehicle traffic, the forgotten dripping of a faucet in the bathroom, the low hum of electronic devices in standby mode, the creak of a door or floor – all compose the home's soundscape and act, silently, on the space's energetic architecture. The mind, even if rationally ignoring these repetitive sounds, absorbs them subliminally as a form of aggression or constant disturbance. It's like trying to meditate or relax deeply with a small stone in your shoe: something always prevents complete immersion in quietude, keeping the nervous system in a subtle state of alert.

The solution for a sonically disharmonious environment doesn't always lie in completely eliminating all sounds. Absolute silence, in certain atmospheres or for certain people, can even be oppressive or uncomfortable. The key lies in sound curation, the conscious introduction of sounds promoting well-being and neutralizing unwanted noises. Healing sounds, especially those mimicking nature, have a remarkable ability to reorganize and elevate the house's vibrational field.

Running water, for example, as mentioned in the previous chapter, carries a sound signature associated with purity, flow, renewal. When present in small indoor fountains (with silent pumps) or well-kept aquariums, it creates a soft, constant auditory backdrop proven to reduce stress levels, increase feelings of freshness and tranquility, and symbolically activate the flow of prosperity and healthy emotions. Wind chimes, when chosen carefully (made of materials producing harmonious sounds, like bamboo, good quality metal, or ceramic) and strategically positioned (usually outdoors like balconies or near windows with a gentle breeze, but never excessively or where the sound becomes irritating), produce light, pleasant resonances. These vibrations help move stagnant Chi, especially in corners, long corridors, or entrances, dispersing stagnant energies and inviting fresh energy to circulate.

Another extremely powerful sound resource is music. But not just any music. Musical selection should be intentional, seeking to harmonize and elevate the home's energy. Soft instrumental music (like piano, classical guitar, harp), Gregorian chants or mantras (carrying spiritual intention and specific vibrations), binaural sounds (designed to induce relaxation or focus states), balanced classical compositions (like Mozart or Bach), or nature music (birdsong, rain, ocean waves) are excellent options. Each room can have its specific soundtrack, adapted to its function and desired energy: in the office, music promoting concentration and mental clarity; in the living room, melodies evoking coziness, relaxation, harmonious conviviality; in the bedroom, deep silences or very soft natural sounds leading to restorative rest.

However, the true healing and harmonizing power of sound resides not only in the external sound source but in the intention and vibration emitted by the residents themselves. When a musical instrument is played with passion and presence, when one sings at home (even off-key, but joyfully), or even when silence is practiced with reverence and mindfulness, something in the space's energetic field purifies and elevates. Sound, in this broader sense, is not just what ears capture, but the intrinsic vibration with which one inhabits a space. Words spoken with love and kindness, laughter shared in joyful moments, prayers murmured with faith at the start of the day or before sleep – all reverberate in the walls, air, objects, imbuing the home with invisible meanings and creating an atmosphere of positivity and welcome.

If sound acts like a wave propagating and moving energy, scent acts like a subtle mist enveloping and penetrating without warning. Smell is one of our most primordial, powerful senses, possessing a direct, immediate connection to the brain's limbic system – the region responsible for processing emotions, memories, instincts. A simple smell can instantly transport us to forgotten childhood moments, evoke a loved one's presence, trigger tears for no apparent reason, or provoke an involuntary smile of pleasure and well-being. A house with its own pleasant, welcoming perfume, reflecting its residents' personality and intention, has already taken a fundamental step towards becoming a true sanctuary, a refuge for body and soul. Scent, like sound, is one of the great sculptors of the invisible in existential Feng Shui. It has the ability to elevate an environment's vibration, energetically purify spaces seeming heavy or charged, induce relaxation or wakefulness states, activate positive memories, stimulate creativity, or silence the agitated mind.

In the quest for an aromatically harmonious home, fragrance choices should follow the principle of naturalness and subtlety. Avoid synthetic odors, overly intense artificial perfumes, or aggressive chemical disinfectants, which often merely mask underlying bad odors and can even carry unbalanced energies or cause allergic reactions. The most beneficial aromas are those emerging from living, natural sources: fresh or dried herbs, freshly cut flowers, aromatic resins from sacred trees, fragrant wood chips, citrus fruit peels. Essential oils, pure, concentrated plant extracts, are one of the most effective, versatile ways to work with aromas at home.

An ultrasonic diffuser with a few drops of lavender essential oil in the bedroom, for example, is a powerful aid for promoting tranquil sleep and reducing anxiety. Citrus oils like sweet orange, lemon, or grapefruit, diffused in the living room or kitchen, help lift spirits, purify the environment, stimulate joy and sociability. Rosemary essential oil, a plant associated with the sun and mental clarity, is indicated for offices (aiding focus) or bathrooms and kitchens (for its fresh scent and purifying properties). Sandalwood, with its woody, deep, spiritual note, is ideal for the home's sacred space, favoring meditation, introspection, connection with the divine.

Incense, used for millennia across various cultures for ritual and therapeutic purposes, also plays an important role in aromatic and energetic harmonization, provided it's of good quality (made with natural resins and herbs, without synthetic additives). Incense smoke, as it rises, not only perfumes the environment but is seen as a vehicle carrying intentions and prayers, purifying space from dense energies and elevating spiritual vibration. Resins like frankincense, myrrh, copal, or breuzinho are particularly powerful for deep energetic cleansings. The aromatic candle, in turn, combines aroma's power with the living presence of the Fire element: its light warms, illuminates, creates an atmosphere of intimacy and presence, while the perfume gently spreads through the air.

The simple act of cooking with natural spices – like cinnamon, clove, ginger, cardamom, nutmeg – also leaves wonderful olfactory traces throughout the house, not only whetting the palate but feeding the spirit with affective memories and feelings of comfort and nourishment. Each room of the house can have its "guiding scent," aligned with its function and desired energy. The kitchen, naturally rich in odors from food preparation, can be balanced with the freshness of herbs like basil or mint in pots, or the citrus aroma of a bowl of lemons and oranges on the counter. The bathroom benefits from scents conveying cleanliness and freshness, like eucalyptus, mint, pine, or tea tree. The living room can receive more welcoming, sociable notes, like resins (frankincense), woods (cedar), or light florals (geranium, ylang-ylang), inviting presence and harmonious conviviality. In the bedroom, scents should be predominantly calming and enveloping, but not overly sedative – lavender, chamomile, marjoram, rose, or jasmine create an atmosphere conducive to relaxation, intimacy, restorative sleep.

However, it's fundamental to remember that before introducing any aroma, something even more important exists: air quality. An environment can have the most exotic, expensive perfumes, but if the air is stale, heavy, stuffy, or laden with humidity and dust, any attempt at aromatic harmonization will be superficial and ineffective. Opening windows daily, allowing cross-ventilation, letting breezes circulate freely, renewing oxygen frequently – all this is as essential, or even more so, than any essential oil or incense. Furthermore, as mentioned, certain indoor plants possess the natural ability to filter air toxins, acting as silent, efficient purifiers.

Sound and scent are, therefore, the invisible threads weaving the house's sensory soul. They are present even when no one consciously perceives them, but their effects on our energy, mood, well-being are profound and undeniable. They don't just decorate space; they inhabit it with a vibrant presence. They are sensitive qualities that can welcome the tired arrival at day's end, lull the sleeper, inspire the creator's gesture, or simply make being at home a richer, more pleasant experience. When adjusted with awareness and intention, sound and scent become silent allies in building a truly living dwelling that speaks to and nourishes all our senses.

And, finally, the secret lies in the fine-tuning between external stimulus and internal listening (or smelling). It's not just about what music is playing, but how that music resonates within you. It's not only about what perfume fills the air, but what memories, emotions, sensations it awakens in your soul. The home managing to tune these subtle frequencies, cultivating a harmonious sound and olfactory landscape, transforms into more than just a physical shelter – it becomes a vibrational field of healing and well-being, where each sound note and aroma molecule collaborate to balance not just the environment, but primarily, the being inhabiting it.

Chapter 19
Intentional Art

Every house reveals a narrative. A silent story manifests through decorative choices, objects resting on shelves, pictures adorning walls. Existential Feng Shui shows us the home as a discreet diary, where everything exposed to the eye unveils fragments of the identity of those residing there. There exists the possibility, profoundly transformative, of deciding with full awareness which stories one wishes to narrate. Art transcends ornamental function, converting into a tool of expression. Space assumes its own language; decoration becomes a mirror reflecting intimate intentions.

Intentional art germinates from the act of observing the environment with presence, questioning: "Does this represent me?" or "Does this speak for me?". Many objects are inheritances, received gifts, impulsive purchases. They occupy prominent places merely out of habit, carrying stories that have lost meaning or, in less favorable scenarios, silently sabotage the house's positive flow. A painting conveying anguish, a forgotten broken statuette, a mirror reflecting what should remain hidden – these seemingly harmless elements construct atmospheres. These atmospheres, in turn, shape daily feelings with greater power than commonly imagined.

A house embracing intentional art breathes truth. It dispenses with rare, expensive pieces or those signed by famous names. The most potent works often arise from manual labor, imbued with affection, memory. A child's drawing, a collage created on an introspective afternoon, a mandala painted as a meditative exercise – anything born from sincere creative gesture already carries authenticity energy, resonating on the soul's frequency. This type of art doesn't aim to impress. It seeks to represent. Representation, in this realm, means tuning symbols with deeply personal meanings. A mountain image might symbolize strength, stability for one person; for another, evoke challenge, overcoming. A bird sculpture might awaken feelings of freedom, lightness, or perhaps nostalgia. Each individual must explore what activates their own symbolic universe. Intention is the master key.

When selecting what to display, reflect on what that object awakens in you through daily contact. Is there beauty? Relief? Connection? Or discomfort, strangeness, weight? This is intentional art's initial filter. A home doesn't function as a neutral gallery. It is a living sanctuary; every element within it should contribute to its daily sacredness, to elevating the spirit of its inhabitant.

The power of each piece's placement is undeniable. Location directly influences the energy the object radiates into the environment and, consequently, into the residents' lives. A symbol of courage, for example, might find its ideal place in the entryway. There, it will function as an invisible guardian, offering strength and protection to both those entering and leaving, marking the threshold between the external world and the personal refuge with an affirmation of determination. A mandala representing balance, with its harmonious, symmetrical geometric forms, could rest above the bed's headboard. Its restorative vibration will act during sleep hours, a period when the subconscious mind is most receptive, promoting tranquil dreams, deep rest, and a more centered awakening. A photograph capturing a genuinely happy moment – a shared smile, a family celebration, a personal achievement – can be strategically positioned to be the first glimpse in the morning. It will function as a morning reminder of gratitude, setting a positive tone even before the day's demands begin to present themselves. Each object's location is, in itself, an act charged with intention, a way of programming the space to support aspirations and well-being.

It's not about overloading environments with a profusion of symbols everywhere. Excess, as explored in various spatial harmonization approaches, tends to stagnate energetic flow, creating visual and mental noise. The quest is for meaningful presence, not accumulation. Fewer pieces, more purpose. The quality of intention surpasses the quantity of objects. A single frame containing inspiring words, carefully chosen for their evocative power, can be more transformative than an entire wall covered with generic images lacking deep personal connection. A candle sculpted with love symbols, like intertwined hearts or infinity knots, can transform a previously forgotten corner of the living room into a focal point of emotional reconnection, a silent reminder of the importance of affective bonds. Intentional art operates through resonance, the quality of energy it emanates, not its ostentation.

The manifestation of intentional art can occur in the subtlest details of daily life. A hand-painted plate with colorful mandalas, used not just for serving but left on the kitchen table as a point of functional beauty. A screen with patterns evoking nature – leaves, bamboo, waves – used to separate rooms, which besides its practical function, evokes a sense of protection, gentle delimitation of spaces. A piece of handmade ceramics, with visible imperfections, a small crack repaired with the *kintsugi* technique (repair with gold), reinforcing Wabi-Sabi's philosophical beauty, celebrating the object's history and resilience. Each visual choice, however small, constitutes an opportunity to narrate, delicately and consciously, the story one wishes to live, the values cherished, the energy one wants to cultivate at home.

It is crucial to remember energy resides not only in the represented form or image. It pulsates potently in the very act of choosing. By selecting a piece because it symbolizes a value you cherish – like love, courage, creativity, faith, joy, silence – the environment begins vibrating at that specific value's frequency. Space becomes a resonant field, amplifying and nurturing that quality in your life. Love can be evoked by images of couples, pinkish colors, objects in pairs. Courage can be represented by figures of strong animals, vibrant red tones, symbols of overcoming. Creativity can be stimulated by abstract art, vivid colors, objects inviting interaction. Faith can be anchored by religious or spiritual symbols, images of light, stones with special meaning. Joy can be brought by solar colors, playful images, objects reminding of happy moments. Silence can be cultivated through minimalist art, neutral colors, representations of tranquil landscapes. These feelings can be evoked through art, not as mere decorative slogans, but as subtle, almost subliminal presences acting in the invisible field, nourishing the soul and directing the home's energy.

Given this, every object deserves to be seen with new eyes, an investigative, present gaze. Do the exercise of walking through your house as if an attentive visitor, curious about the story that space tells. Observe what hangs on walls, rests on furniture, accumulates in corners. Ask yourself honestly: does this object represent something I still wish to cultivate in my life? Does it resonate with who I am today? Or is it just an echo of a time already passed, a reminder of a pain already overcome, a fragment of a version of me left behind, no longer relevant to my current path? Radical honesty in this personal analysis is the fundamental first step to transforming decoration, previously perhaps automatic or inherited, into a powerful act of healing, alignment, conscious creation of one's own environment.

By opening physical space, by gratefully removing what no longer resonates with your present energy, a fertile field is created for new pieces, new symbols, new intentions to emerge and find place.

There's no need to fill this space immediately. Emptiness itself is also a potent act of intention. Leaving a wall free can mean openness to the new, availability for the unknown, trust in life's flow. A minimalist altar, containing only a stone found in nature and a fresh flower, can hold more symbolic potency, more energetic strength, than dozens of objects accumulated without clear purpose, merely filling space. An environment's emotional clarity begins with discernment, the ability to choose what stays and what goes, based not on external rules, but on inner listening and heart's resonance.

For those feeling the call to create their own pieces, the home also transforms into a studio, a laboratory for soul expression. No formal artistic skills or considering oneself an "artist" in the conventional sense are needed. Just be true to oneself. Painting, drawing, making collages with magazine cutouts or old photos, writing poems and displaying them in simple frames, composing a short piece of music and letting it play softly occasionally – all these actions activate the creative force inherent in every human being. This creative force, once awakened and expressed, radiates through the house like a soft light, a vibrant, authentic energy. What is born from hands with affection, intention, presence, remains in the environment as a blessing, a personal energetic signature elevating the space's vibration.

Intentional art need not be literal or figurative. It can be abstract, symbolic, geometric. What's crucial is that it represents something the resident recognizes as theirs, part of their inner language. A spiral might symbolize continuous growth, evolution, journey. A circle might represent union, totality, cycles. A simple dot in the center of a canvas could be the manifestation of the silence you wish to cultivate amidst the world's incessant noise. When the need to please others' eyes, follow fleeting trends, is abandoned, true authentic expression emerges. It's this genuine expression that fills the house with soul, personality, life.

Even purely functional objects can carry an artistic, intentional dimension. A lampshade made of handmade paper, filtering light softly, organically. Coasters with geometric patterns evoking nature or sacred symbols. A lampshade whose glass you painted yourself, on a creative afternoon. Everything can carry intention, if chosen, modified, or created so. Art then ceases to be an isolated category, restricted to paintings and sculptures, and permeates daily life in an integrated way. A bath towel embroidered with symbols you love, transforming a routine act into a small ritual. A small sculpture, perhaps representing a power animal, hidden on the bookshelf like a personal secret, a discreet source of strength. A collection of stones found on meaningful trips, arranged on a tray as tactile reminders of the path traveled, experiences lived.

Thus, the home becomes a living portrait not of what you materially possess, but of who you are in essence. Or, more precisely, of who you are becoming each day. With each new conscious choice, each replacement of an object that lost meaning with another resonating with the present moment, each symbol placed with presence and intention, you actively shape the environment. Space begins to inspire you, welcome you, subtly direct you on your growth path. The house transforms simultaneously into compass and nest. Not only protecting physically but guiding energetically. In the eloquent silence of forms, in colors vibrating on walls like musical notes, in textures eyes caress even before hands touch them, art reveals itself as a silent prayer, a continuous visual meditation. The home, then, transforms into a daily altar. A place where routine is permeated with sacredness, where each object speaks the soul's deep language, where every displayed image reveals the path unfolding from inside out. This is the transformative proposal of intentional art: making visible, in the external environment, what, within you, wishes to be remembered, nurtured, celebrated every day. Not to impress others, not to follow fads. But to not forget yourself, to anchor your truth in the space you call home.

Chapter 20
Free Space

An invisible presence permeates many houses, frequently unnoticed. It hides behind unused furniture, rests in drawers cluttered with forgotten papers, hovers over closets sheltering clothes that no longer fit the body or the soul. It is stagnation. It settles in subtly, transforming what seemed like simple accumulation into a true energetic prison, limiting the vital flow in the environment and in the residents' lives. The absence of free space reveals more than an aesthetic problem; it is a direct reflection of the human difficulty in letting go, releasing the past, trusting in what's to come.

Creating free space is, fundamentally, an act of courage. Emptiness, for many, is frightening. It confronts us with life's impermanence, the future's uncertainty, the discomfort of not knowing what will come to fill that place. This is why so many people prefer to keep objects that have completely lost meaning: they represent a story that, though concluded, still offers the illusion of control, of security in the known. A house filled with excess does not welcome the new. It transforms into a museum of the resident's past versions, a dusty archive of identities no longer serving. No being can truly grow, evolve, while inhabiting the setting of a time already gone, energetically bound to outdated circumstances.

Existential Feng Shui treats free space as sacred territory, essential for vitality. It is there, in the voids, in unobstructed areas, that Chi, vital energy, circulates fully, renewing and nourishing the environment. It is in emptiness that the home's breath is felt, that the environment can freely inhale and exhale. Just as the physical body needs pauses between movements to maintain balance, catch its breath, the domestic environment needs intervals, visual respites, energetic clearings to sustain harmony. Free space is, in essence, living, pulsating space, full of potential.

It's not about emptying for emptying's sake, seeking sterile or impersonal minimalism. The proposal lies not in imposing an external aesthetic ideal, but in attentive listening to the house, sensitive perception of where excess suffocates, where energy feels blocked, where the environment cries out for liberation. A bookshelf crammed with books never to be reread, accumulating dust and silent guilt, can become an invisible weight, an anchor preventing the flow of new ideas. A shelf filled with trinkets no longer communicating anything to the heart, having lost their charm or meaning, blocks the gaze, tires the mind. A closet overflowing with clothes no longer reflecting who you are today, belonging to previous life phases, restricts movements, not just physically when looking for what to wear, but also existentially, preventing expression of current identity.

The practice of decluttering, when performed with clear intention and presence, reveals itself as one of the most powerful forms of energetic transmutation available domestically. Each object consciously removed, with gratitude for service rendered, represents a corresponding internal release. By opening physical space externally, mental and emotional space simultaneously opens internally. It's like releasing invisible moorings, one by one, allowing the soul to float lighter, freer to explore new horizons. It's not uncommon that after a major cleanup and organization, unexpected insights arise, decisions long postponed become crystal clear, and even sleep quality significantly deepens. The space opening up in the house is the same space opening up in the mind, heart, life's possibilities.

This release process, however, needs to be conducted with deep respect for one's own history and involved emotions. Some objects carry dense layers of emotional meaning, memories of important times, affections woven in the silence of family or personal recollections. One should not force the release of anything still genuinely alive within you, still positively nourishing your soul somehow. Honesty with oneself is crucial. Keeping a gift from someone with whom a painful bond was broken, for example, can be an invisible thread binding you energetically to that past suffering, preventing healing and openness to new relationships. Conserving broken objects, piled in a corner with the vague excuse of fixing them "someday," might be an unconscious metaphor for one's own feeling of inadequacy, difficulty dealing with the "broken parts" of oneself one wishes to avoid confronting.

What no longer serves, what has completed its cycle, needs to depart so the new can arrive. This doesn't represent carelessness towards the past or lack of respect for history; on the contrary, it's an act of reverence for the future, a vote of confidence in life's continuity. It's declaring, through concrete, symbolic gestures, that there is space in your life for what is yet to come, for new experiences, new people, new opportunities. That you trust life's intrinsic abundance and no longer need to hoard things out of fear of scarcity, fear that something might be lacking. This is one of accumulation's biggest psychological and energetic traps: the limiting belief that if you don't keep everything, you'll inevitably face lack. True abundance flow, on all levels, establishes itself when one cultivates faith that the essential will always find its way to you, that the universe provides what's necessary at the right time.

Start small, so as not to feel overwhelmed. Choose a drawer. A specific shelf. A box of old papers. Look item by item, holding each in your hands if necessary. Ask sincerely: does this still represent me? Does it still have practical use or relevant meaning in my current life? Does it still bring me joy to look at or use? If the answer is a clear "no" to all or most of these questions, thank the object for the function it fulfilled and let it go. Donate to someone who might need it, recycle if applicable, pass it on to friends or family who might value it. If the object is broken, ask yourself with absolute honesty if it will really be fixed in the near future. If the answer is uncertain or negative, perhaps it's time to discard it. If it's irreversibly stained, torn beyond repair, expired, perhaps it's just waiting for your courage to let it go, to release the physical and energetic space it occupies.

As physical space gradually opens up, a new perspective on oneself and one's real needs begins to emerge. You start noticing, perhaps surprisingly, that you don't need so many things to feel whole, secure, or happy. That energy flows much better, both in the environment and in your own life, with fewer physical and mental obstacles. That beauty often reveals itself in the nuances of emptiness, simplicity, clarity. And that the house, upon being freed from the superfluous, begins breathing more softly, lightly, becoming a more welcoming, revitalizing environment.

Free space isn't restricted only to visible areas of the house. It's equally necessary in hidden spaces: inside closets, deep drawers, storage rooms, garages, or that "junk room." That room in the back, often full of boxes whose contents you don't even remember, carries a particularly dense, stagnant energetic charge. It functions as a shadow zone in the home, a physical repository for postponed thoughts, the "I'll deal with it later," the "someday I'll use it," the "I don't want to deal with this now." Each of these thoughts, even operating unconsciously, generates a subtle blockage in the house's overall flow – and, by reflection, in life's own flow.

In Feng Shui, clutter, accumulated disorder, holds considerable vibrational weight. It tends to lower the environment's energetic frequency, generate stagnation, hinder healthy Chi circulation. It prevents vital energy from moving lightly, nourishingly, clearly. By opening space in these forgotten places, one isn't just physically cleaning – one is primarily clearing the stagnant energy accumulated there, releasing old patterns, trapped emotions, unfinished projects draining vitality. Often, upon completely emptying a previously cluttered room, a palpable change in atmosphere can be perceived: a different smell in the air, light seeming brighter than before, or even an inexplicable physical sensation of relief, as if a weight has been lifted from the shoulders.

Creating and maintaining free space also involves a conscious reassessment of consumption and attachment habits. Buying on impulse, accumulating objects without real need or meaning, having difficulty detaching from what has clearly fulfilled its function. All contribute to saturating the house, blocking flow. A home in vibrational harmony isn't one filled with beautiful or expensive things, but one where everything present has a clear why, a defined function, personal meaning. Where there's space for the eye to rest without being bombarded by excessive information, for the body to move freely without bumping into obstacles, for the spirit to feel truly at home, welcomed by clarity and order.

However, this conquered space needs to be maintained. Decluttering shouldn't be seen as an isolated event, an arduous task performed once. It's a continuous practice, a state of attention and care. Something done regularly, with love, discernment, lightness. Each change of season, a new cycle begins, offering a natural opportunity to review closets, drawers, objects. Each significant internal change – a new job, end of a relationship, new life phase – necessitates a new external review to align the environment with the present moment. The house should accompany your personal evolution. And for that, it needs to be always ready to change with you, reflect who you are now.

There is also symbolic free space – the kind not perceived with physical eyes but felt with the soul. A purposefully empty corner can be an invitation to contemplation, meditation, inner silence. A wall without pictures, broad and clear, can function as a necessary pause for a mind overloaded with stimuli. A floor free of rugs or excess furniture can be an invitation to spontaneous movement, dance, bodily expression. Visual silence deeply calms the senses. And it's in this silence, this fertile void, that intuition flourishes, the inner voice makes itself heard more clearly.

By releasing the house from material excess, you simultaneously free yourself from automatic behavioral repetitions, emotional attachments no longer making sense, unconscious fears preventing life's natural flow. You declare, through organizing your physical space, that you are open to living lighter, more consciously, more connected to the present moment.

Ultimately, free space is not synonymous with absence or deprivation. It is, in fact, expanded presence. It is the fertile territory where the new can germinate, where opportunities can find place to manifest. It is the invisible altar of trust in life. Because only those trusting the universe's intrinsic abundance can let go, with gratitude, of what has already played its part. And when this trust deeply settles in, the home radically transforms. It ceases to be a mere repository of objects accumulated over time and becomes a vibrant field of possibilities. Energy circulates freely. The gaze rests. The body relaxes. The mind breathes relieved. The heart opens. In this rediscovered, cultivated free space, resides freedom. And with it, life can dance in its fullest, lightest, most authentic form.

Chapter 21
Energetic Cleansing

The energy of a house transcends its physical walls. It is not limited to the arranged furniture, nor even to the air circulating through the rooms. It subtly infiltrates crevices, rests in the most forgotten corners, reverberates in objects laden with history, extending like an invisible field, an aura embracing each environment. When physical space is touched by intense emotions, striking memories, significant events, it absorbs these marks like a silent mirror, recording the vibrations of everything occurring there. Energetic cleansing emerges, in this context, as an essential ritual of rebirth for the home. It not only removes accumulated subtle residues, dense or stagnant energies, but returns the house to its essential purity, its original vibration, allowing it to once again be a sanctuary of peace and vitality.

Living is a continuous act of overflowing energy. The joy echoing in contagious laughter, the silent weeping of a difficult dawn, paralyzing fear, explosive anger, enchantment before beauty. Every emotion felt and expressed within the home leaves an energetic trace in the environment. Just as dust physically accumulates on furniture, emotional and mental charges settle in the invisible layers of space, creating an atmosphere that can become heavy or disharmonious over time. It is for this reason that certain houses, even when impeccably clean and physically organized, feel heavy, oppressive. And others, even very simple and modest, welcome like a warm hug, transmitting an immediate sense of well-being. The difference lies in the energetic frequency vibrating there – a frequency that can, fortunately, be consciously renewed and elevated.

It is not necessary for something serious or traumatic to have happened to justify performing an energetic cleanse. The very dynamic of daily life, with its natural ups and downs, moves emotional waves that constantly imprint upon the space. Interpersonal conflicts, periods of illness, significant losses, but also profound internal changes like relationship endings, beginnings of new cycles, personal rebirths – all leave energetic traces. Energetic cleansing is a subtle, deep act of care. It not only cleanses what is dense but honors the house's natural cycle, recognizing its capacity to absorb and transform. It is comparable to pruning a plant so it grows more vigorously, or opening all windows after a long winter to renew the air. It is an act of revitalization.

There are many traditional and contemporary ways to energetically cleanse an environment. None is intrinsically "more right" than another. Effectiveness lies less in the specific technique and more in the presence of the one performing it. The clear intention to purify and elevate energy, the heart involved in the process, the genuine connection with the space. It is this internal vibrational field of the practitioner that activates the transformative power of each gesture, each element used. What follows are just possible paths, suggestions based on different traditions. But it is the state of consciousness while treading them that makes them truly sacred and effective.

Smudging is perhaps the most ancient and universal of spatial purification rituals. Burning dried herbs is an act practiced by countless cultures around the world since time immemorial. Ancient peoples did it around sacred fires, in important rites of passage, to mark births, honor deaths, celebrate harvests, perform healings. The smoke rising from smoldering herbs is seen as a visual prayer, a vehicle carrying cleansing intentions to subtle planes. It has the ability to transform the dense into light, the stagnant into fluid. White sage, known for its intense purifying properties; rosemary, associated with protection and mental clarity; lavender, bringing calm and harmony; rue, traditionally used to ward off negative energies; myrrh and frankincense, sacred resins used for spiritual elevation – each plant carries its own vibrational signature, its own purification codes. By burning a bundle of these herbs or resins and walking through the house, intentionally guiding the smoke through all corners, doors, windows, and high-traffic areas, it is as if we were painting the air with a new light, dissolving energetic shadows.

However, it's not just about lighting the herbs and walking through the house mechanically. The ritual's soul resides in the conscious gesture, full presence. Before starting, take a moment to breathe deeply. Connect with the intention of what you wish to cleanse:

it could be a specific weight felt in a room's air, a recurring feeling of tiredness or irritability, an inexplicable stagnation in some area of life reflected in the home. As you pass the smoke, visualize or feel it dissolving and transmuting everything that no longer serves the harmony of the space and its residents. Visualize it making space for lightness, clarity, love, prosperity to enter. Repeat mentally or softly a phrase, affirmation, or prayer resonating with your heart, like "May all dense energy be transmuted into light" or "This house is clean, protected, and blessed." Or simply remain silent, allowing the plant's wisdom to act through the smoke, trusting its purification capacity.

Another powerful instrument for energetic cleansing is sound. Like smoke, sound vibrations penetrate where physical eyes cannot reach. Sound vibrates, moves, breaks patterns of stagnant energy. Simple practices like clapping vigorously in room corners, ringing bells with clear, high-pitched sound, shaking an indigenous rattle or maraca, or sounding a Tibetan or crystal singing bowl can be very effective. Each sound has the power to dislodge trapped energies, creating movement and dispersing density. House corners, especially darker ones, difficult to access, or little used, tend to accumulate stagnant energy, forming "pockets" of stagnation. By emitting sounds at these specific points, intending to break these blockages, you are disrupting subtle patterns, opening cracks for energetic renewal to flow.

Sound can also be vibrated through one's own voice. Chanting a sacred mantra with devotion (like

"Om"), singing a prayer or hymn with faith, or even repeating a simple "thank you" or "I love you" with intention directed towards the space. All this echoes in the walls, in the home's energetic field, and transforms it. The house listens. It absorbs the vibration of words, sounds. And responds with a lighter, elevated atmosphere.

Water, universally associated with purification and flow, can also be used powerfully in energetic cleansing. Sprinkling a simple mixture of water and coarse salt throughout the rooms is one of the most accessible, effective practices. Salt, a natural crystal formed in the earth, has the intrinsic ability to absorb dense, negative energies, neutralizing the environment and returning the space to its original vibrational neutrality. One can prepare a solution by mixing filtered water (or rainwater, if possible) with a handful of coarse salt (preferably unrefined) in a clean spray bottle. Walk through the rooms gently spraying the mixture, paying special attention to doors, windows, baseboards, corners, and objects seeming to carry many memories or heavy energies. Some people prefer placing small containers (like saucers or small cups) with coarse salt at strategic points in the house, such as room corners or under furniture like the bed or sofa. Leave it there for a few days (usually 3 to 7 days) for the salt to absorb dense energies, then discard the contents preferably onto the earth (so the energy is transmuted) or in running water (like flushing down the toilet, visualizing the energy going away). This simple, ancestral gesture functions as an invitation to the space's energetic rebirth:

the old is absorbed and released, allowing the new to emerge with more clarity and vitality.

Light also possesses purifying properties. A candle lit with clear intention of cleansing and elevation functions as a miniature sun within the home, bringing warmth, light, transmutation. One can light a white candle (color associated with purity and peace) in each room, one at a time, dedicating a few moments to silence, feel the space's energy, intend purification. It's not just about physically illuminating, but re-enchanting the space, bringing the living presence of the fire element to dissolve energetic shadows. The living, dancing flame has the power to break patterns and elevate vibration. It's also possible to use aromatic candles, thus combining the fire element with the therapeutic power of essential oils, choosing scents like sage, rosemary, or lavender to enhance cleansing.

Some use the power of crystals, positioning them strategically in places where denser or disharmonious energy is felt. Clear quartz (or rock crystal) is known for its ability to cleanse and amplify energies. Amethyst transmutes negative energies into positive ones and promotes spirituality. Black tourmaline is a powerful protector against dense and electromagnetic energies. Each stone possesses a specific vibration and acts as a silent guardian of the space's energy. It's important to remember to cleanse and energize crystals regularly, for example, by washing them in running water, leaving them under full moonlight or sunlight (depending on the crystal), or burying them in the earth for a few hours so they renew and continue acting effectively.

And perhaps the most powerful, simplest of all methods is simply opening everything. Opening windows, curtains, doors. Letting the sun enter generously. Letting the wind run freely through the house. Nature is the greatest healer. When an environment is invaded by abundant natural light and circulating fresh air, something fundamental reorganizes in its energetic field. Chi begins moving vigorously again. Walls seem to breathe. The house awakens from its lethargy.

Beyond all methods and tools, there is a fundamental secret. The deepest, most lasting energetic cleansing is performed with genuine love for the space. When one walks through an environment expressing gratitude – for the shelter it offers, the history it holds, the lessons it teaches, the silences it welcomes – the vibrational field instantly elevates. Gratitude purifies. More potently than any external ritual performed mechanically.

After cleansing, it's important to seal the new energetic cycle, marking the fresh start. This can be done simply: with a soft, natural scent in the air, an aroma diffuser with essential oils bringing joy or peace (like orange or geranium), a small renewed altar with a fresh flower and a lit candle, soft, elevated music playing in the background. Each person will intuitively know how to mark this restart meaningfully for themselves. What matters is that the gesture is felt, conscious. Not automatic. That it celebrates the space now free, now renewed, now ready to support life's next movement with more harmony and vitality.

The house, like the body, needs care rituals. Not because it intrinsically sickens, but because it lives, breathes, absorbs. And everything living, changes. Everything changing, accumulates cycles needing closure. Everything undergoing a process of conscious cleansing becomes sacred again. By making energetic cleansing a recurring practice – perhaps with each season change, after important events, or whenever feeling heaviness or stagnation – the home becomes more than a physical space. It becomes a living temple. And within it, the inhabitant also gradually transforms. Because it's not just the environment changing with these rituals. It's the being perceiving itself increasingly connected to everything around, sensitive to subtle energies. It's the being slowly learning that cleansing the house is also a powerful way to cleanse one's own soul. And, in this deep encounter between the invisible and the daily gesture, the true magic of conscious presence in the home is born.

Chapter 22
Harmonious Entrance

A house's energy doesn't begin abruptly upon crossing the threshold. It starts forming much earlier, on the path leading to the door, in how the boundary between the external world and the inner refuge is presented and cared for. The entrance is this crucial transition point, the place where Chi, universal vital energy, makes its first direct contact with the home. How this initial passage is organized, decorated, lit, and maintained reveals — and, in a way, determines — much of the energetic quality experienced in the internal rooms. A harmonious entrance transcends mere aesthetics; it is profoundly symbolic. It communicates to the universe, to arriving visitors, and primarily, to the resident upon returning, the quality of presence, welcome, and care one wishes to cultivate within one's own life.

Some houses, at first glance, invite, welcome. The sound of footsteps in the hallway seems to naturally slow down, the air around the door feels lighter, shoulders relax almost involuntarily. In other residences, even before the door opens, a silent discomfort is perceived — objects piled on the path, clutter accumulated on the porch or hall, lack of adequate lighting, a palpable absence of welcoming energy. One doesn't need deep technical knowledge of Feng Shui to feel when an entrance portal is energetically imbalanced. The body perceives it instantly. Vital energy, Chi, hesitates to enter.

In Feng Shui, the main door is often called the "mouth of Chi." It's through it that the main energy current enters to feed and nourish the entire house. If this entrance is somehow blocked, physically or energetically, if neglected, dirty, or disordered, the Chi flow will inevitably be weakened right at the source. Internal rooms, consequently, will reflect this initial blockage subtly but constantly, manifesting as feelings of stagnation, lack of vitality, or difficulty realizing projects. It's like trying to breathe deeply through a narrow, bent straw: oxygen reaches the lungs, but not with the fullness and strength needed to revitalize the entire organism.

Building harmony at the entrance starts by ensuring free space. The path leading to the door should be completely clear, allowing a smooth, fluid approach. Avoid placing overly large plant pots obstructing passage, exposed trash cans bringing disposal energy near the entrance, broken or disused objects, or any elements causing a feeling of tightness, constriction. The journey home needs to be like a river calmly approaching its source, inviting tranquility. The lightness of this path prepares the vibrational field of both visitor and resident for the transition to the internal space, signaling an environment of peace and order.

Cleanliness is another absolutely essential point. Dusty doors, with cobwebs in corners, dirty or worn entrance mats, adjacent external areas abandoned or poorly maintained not only indicate physical neglect but also retain dense, stagnant energy, preventing fresh, new energy from entering easily. Cleaning the door regularly, keeping glass (if any) shining, sweeping the sidewalk, access corridor, or porch are gestures that, beyond their obvious practical function, act as powerful energetic renewal rituals. With each intentional cleaning, stagnant energy is shaken off, released, and the entrance's vibrational field reorganizes, becoming more receptive and luminous.

Caring for lighting also radically transforms the entrance's energy. Dim lights, burnt-out bulbs, or the complete absence of adequate lighting in the external area drain the space's vitality, conveying a sense of abandonment, insecurity, or melancholy. Good outdoor lighting, conversely, transmits security, welcome, presence, care. It doesn't need to be excessively intense or expensive; just bright enough to well illuminate the path and door, functional, and ideally, constant during the night. A soft, warm light lit at the entrance during the night can function as an internal beacon, a signal guiding and welcoming, silently communicating: "here is life, here is beauty, here is care."

What is positioned directly in front of the main door also matters significantly. Avoid accumulating disposable objects like trash bags (even temporarily), debris from small renovations, or any element representing disorganization, decay, or Sha (negative) energy. If there's a plant decorating the entrance, ensure it's alive, healthy, well-cared-for. A dying or sick plant at the entrance can symbolize blockages or difficulties. If there's furniture, like a bench or console table, ensure it's clean, in good condition, and ideally, has a clear function (like holding keys or mail). This immediate contact point between exterior and interior should express the quality of life, order, beauty one wishes to nurture within the home.

We arrive, then, at the door itself. It represents much more than a simple security item or structural component of the house. It is a powerful symbol of passage, opportunity, connection between worlds. It should open easily, completely, without annoying squeaks, without obstacles behind it preventing its full opening. Doors that jam, require force to open, or hit furniture when opened, symbolically represent energetic blockages, difficulties receiving new opportunities, obstacles in life's flow. The gesture of opening the door to enter the house needs to be fluid, easy, almost ritualistic: upon opening the home, one also opens the heart, opens the flow for vital energy to enter.

Door colors also communicate specific energies. In traditional Feng Shui, each cardinal direction has recommended colors for the entrance door, based on Five Elements theory (e.g., North-facing doors might benefit from blue or black, associated with Water; East-facing doors from green or brown, linked to Wood). Beyond these correspondences, it's important to choose tones conveying the desired feeling for arrivals. Dark tones like black, navy blue, or burgundy, when well-maintained and in good condition, can evoke depth, protection, mystery. Light or vibrant colors like white, yellow, red, or light green tend to call for lightness, joy, vitality. Most importantly, the door should always be clean, without visible cracks, with intact, well-maintained paint. If possible, personalize it with a touch representing residents' identity: a welcome wreath (renewed seasonally), a discreet protection symbol (like a Greek eye or Bagua), a clearly visible, beautiful number, an ornament bringing joy.

The entrance mat also plays a more significant role than just cleaning shoes. It symbolically represents transition – the act of leaving the world's energies outside to step onto the home's sacred ground. Therefore, its choice and maintenance deserve attention. It should be beautiful, clean, whole, without tears or excessive wear. Mats with positive phrases ("Welcome," "Home Sweet Home"), auspicious symbols (like the infinity knot or mandalas), or simply a color evoking well-being and welcome can be great allies at this energetic crossing point. It's fundamental to keep it always clean – a worn, stained, grimy mat retains exactly the kind of dense, dirty energy one wants to avoid bringing into the house.

The immediate interior of the door, the first glimpse upon entering, is another key point for harmony. Upon opening the door and taking the first step inside, what does one see first? A white, empty, cold wall? A coat rack crammed with disorganized coats, bags, shoes? A piece of furniture cluttered with mail and random objects? All communicate an immediate energetic message. Ideally, the first look upon entering the house should be of harmony, beauty, order. It could be an inspiring painting with an image bringing peace, a thriving living plant in a beautiful pot, an intentional art piece representing family values, or simply a free, well-lit space. What matters is a feeling of clarity, welcome, breath.

The entrance hall, when existing as a defined room or space, functions as an invitation to conscious transition between exterior and interior. It physically separates the public world from the home's private, intimate universe. For this very reason, it's a space deserving special attention in its decoration and energy. It shouldn't be seen as temporary storage for objects or a neglected passageway, but as an energetic portal. An elegant console table with fresh flowers or a beautiful plant, a carefully positioned mirror (never directly reflecting the entrance door), a diffuser with a soft, welcoming scent – all help set the home's energetic tone right upon arrival.

Mirrors, incidentally, deserve particular emphasis at the entrance. In Feng Shui, placing a mirror directly opposite the main door is generally discouraged, as it's believed it can "push" Chi back out, preventing vital energy from entering and circulating through the house. However, placed laterally on one of the hall walls, a mirror can be very beneficial: it visually expands the entrance, reflects light (natural or artificial), and creates a feeling of greater space and welcome. Everything depends on strategic position and the intention behind its use.

Wind chimes, mobiles gently moving with air currents, or other elements producing delicate sounds are also welcome in the entrance area (whether outside on the porch, or just inside the door, in the hall). They activate stagnant Chi, break patterns of stopped energy, and sonically mark the portal between external and internal worlds. A bell gently sounding upon opening the door can function as a subtle greeting to incoming energy, a sonic reminder of transition. The sound should be pleasant, discreet, and the object itself clean, well-positioned, harmonically tuned.

Caring for the entrance is, in essence, caring for the house's energetic narrative. It's consciously deciding how the story begins each time someone – visitor or resident – crosses the threshold. It's communicating to the universe and oneself: "here one enters with respect, lightness, presence." It's reminding oneself, every day upon returning, that life happens in a continuous exchange between outside and inside, and the essential meeting point is this small yet powerful entrance portal.

If the house lacks a formal hall, if the door opens directly into the living room or another room, it becomes even more important to symbolically create this transition zone. This can be done with a rug of different shape or color defining the entrance area, specific lighting at this point, a delicate screen creating a soft visual barrier, or even an arrangement of significant objects on furniture near the door. What's important is marking the arrival point, where the pause between "out there" and "in here" occurs. Body and spirit need this demarcation, this energetic key change.

In the end, the harmonious entrance is not just the physical beginning of the house. It is the beginning of everything in terms of energy flow. It's where the subtle boundary between the potential chaos of the outside world and the protective intimacy of being is crossed. It's where one unconsciously decides if incoming energy will be well-received and circulate freely, or meet resistance and get lost in initial friction. And, above all, it's where the resident reconnects with themselves, day after day, turning the key, opening the door, entering the sacred space that is their home. May each arrival be a conscious return to your center. May each entrance be a silent blessing. May the house, starting at the door, always be the luminous, welcoming mirror of who you truly are.

Chapter 23
Harmonious Living Room

The living room occupies a central position in the home's dynamic, transcending the function of a simple room. It is the visible heart of the house, the stage where the presences of residents and visitors intersect, where comfortable silences are shared without need for words, where meaningful conversations build bridges between intimate worlds. In its deepest essence, the living room represents the primary setting for social and family interactions, restorative pauses, spontaneous encounters requiring no appointment or formality. Like any pulsating heart, its energetic and functional health directly influences the well-being of the entire organism that is the home. If harmony vibrates in this central space, there is vital pulse, life circulating vigorously and purposefully through all other rooms of the house.

A truly harmonious living room is not defined by its physical size, ostentatious luxury furniture, or adherence to the latest market-dictated decorative trends. It is recognized, primarily, by the feeling it evokes in those who enter. Upon entering, the body instinctively relaxes. Eyes find points of visual rest, without being bombarded by excess information. The spirit settles, feeling safe and welcomed. There is an intangible atmosphere, difficult to explain in words but easily perceptible on the skin: the space invites permanence without being invasive; welcomes without suffocating; inspires without agitating. It's a delicate balance between comfort, beauty, and energetic functionality.

Building this desired harmony begins with the careful arrangement of elements in the space. Furniture arrangement, in particular, determines not only aesthetics but primarily the flow of Chi – vital energy – and, consequently, the flow of communication and interaction among people using the room. Sofas and armchairs positioned to face each other, creating a conversation circle or semi-circle, suggest dialogue, reciprocity, active listening. This configuration encourages eye contact, idea exchange, experience sharing. Conversely, an arrangement where all furniture faces exclusively towards a television set indicates dispersed centrality, focused on passive entertainment, where human interaction tends to lose strength and priority. The ideal, in most cases, is to seek functional and energetic balance: the screen can be present, as part of modern life, but should not completely dominate the room or be the sole focus. It should remain in waiting mode, silent when unused, while real exchanges, meaningful conversations, happen around it, perhaps in a secondary seating arrangement or simply through flexible use.

Circulation within the living room also needs respect and facilitation. Paths obstructed by poorly positioned furniture, excessively tight passages between pieces, furniture disproportionate to the room's actual size (either too large, causing a cramped feeling, or too small, seeming lost in space) create energetic barriers that, even if often imperceptible consciously, affect overall well-being. The human body likes flowing through space without bumping, without feeling constrained. And Chi, vital energy, follows the same principle, seeking free, smooth paths. Therefore, observe attentively how you move within your living room. Is there natural fluidity? Are there constant interruptions on the path? Does any specific area seem instinctively avoided by you or others? These silent answers, observed attentively, reveal where space cries out for adjustment, release, reorganization allowing more harmonious flow.

Colors chosen for the living room play another important layer in creating the desired atmosphere. Earthy tones (like browns, beiges, ochres), neutral beiges, soft greens (reminiscent of nature and calming), or muted oranges (bringing warmth without agitation) tend to convey a sense of coziness, stability, comfort. However, there's no absolute, universal rule. Everything depends on the specific vibration desired in that space and the residents' personality. More vibrant colors, like yellows, reds, or intense blues, used moderately, can stimulate livelier encounters, more vivid conversations, a more festive atmosphere. Predominantly neutral tones, on the other hand, favor introspection, calm, a more serene, contemplative environment. A balanced combination, often, is key to accommodating different moments and moods experienced in the living room. A touch of vibrant red in a decorative cushion, a painting with deep blue tones on a neutral wall, a mustard-colored throw casually draped over the sofa – these are small chromatic insertions activating energy, bringing personality, but not dominating or overwhelming the environment.

Texture is another vital aspect, frequently underestimated, in creating a welcoming living room. Soft-to-touch fabrics (like velvet, chenille, wool, combed cotton), thick, inviting rugs urging bare feet, generous blankets and cushions seeming to embrace the body – all contribute to the room being felt tactilely, sensorially, not just appreciated visually. A living room shouldn't just look cozy in photographs; it needs to be lived as such daily. Touch, in this context, transforms into a silent language of affection, comfort, care, communicating to the body that this is a safe place to relax and surrender. Materials like natural wood, stone, ceramic, and plant fibers (like sisal, jute, wicker) also contribute their unique textures to enrich the space's sensory experience.

Natural elements are always welcome and highly recommended for bringing life and balance to the living room. A larger plant positioned in a strategic corner, filling vertical space. Green leaves moving gently with the breeze from the window, bringing a sense of natural movement. A vase with fresh, colorful flowers on the coffee or console table, renewing energy and bringing ephemeral beauty. Nature, when introduced into the built environment, breaks rigidity, introduces the organic rhythm of the natural world into the often sterile linearity of concrete and industrialized materials. And this, invariably, heals, calms, reconnects. Even a single plant, provided it's well-cared-for and healthy, can significantly change the environment's energetic frequency. The presence of green balances vital energy (Chi), helps purify the air (in some cases), softens architectural forms, and invites calm, contemplation.

Lighting, as in other rooms, demands sensitivity and planning in the living room. Excessively white, intense lights, typical of commercial settings, can over-agitate, create a cold, impersonal atmosphere. Very dim or poorly distributed lights, conversely, can obscure the space's vitality, making it gloomy or melancholic. Ideally, there should be different light points, with varying intensities and color temperatures, activated and combined according to moment and need. General lighting, perhaps ceiling-mounted, for more active moments or receiving guests. Softer, lower yellow light from lamps or sconces to create a cozy mood in late afternoon or evening. A lit candle or a lamp with very delicate light for nighttime conversations, relaxation moments, or watching a movie. Light, when well-positioned and controlled, has the power to draw distinct atmospheres within the same space. And each created atmosphere communicates and induces a specific internal state.

The center of the living room, from a Feng Shui perspective, is often considered a point of energy concentration and distribution, related to health and overall balance (associated with the Earth element in the Bagua). Ideally, it should be relatively free, clean, allowing energy to breathe and circulate without obstructions. It doesn't need to be completely empty, but it's essential it's not weighed down by very large furniture or excess objects. A low coffee table of appropriate proportions, perhaps with few significant objects on it (a book, a candle, a small floral arrangement), a rug defining the seating area without visually trapping it, a space where the eye can rest peacefully without interruption from excessive visual information – all contribute to the stability and harmony of the living room's energetic center.

Walls tell silent stories through what's displayed on them. And here again enters the importance of intentional art, as explored previously, but applied specifically to the home's social heart. Paintings visually representing desired feelings and cultivations in that space – peace (tranquil landscapes), joy (vibrant colors, playful scenes), unity (group images, mandalas). Photographs bringing up happy, significant family or friend memories. Wall textures (like wood, stone, or fabric cladding) reminding of nature's welcoming touch. It's important to avoid images conveying dense feelings (sadness, anguish, loneliness), excessive abstract art potentially causing mental confusion, or elements bringing conflicting emotions or unpleasant memories. What's on the walls constantly enters through the eyes and subtly reverberates in the occupants' body and emotional field.

Also avoid generalized object accumulation. Shelves packed with books and souvenirs lacking current meaning, bookcases filled with decorative items just to fill space, side or coffee tables with excess adornments. The human eye needs respites, visual pauses to avoid fatigue. Emptiness is as important as object presence; it functions as the invisible frame valuing what was chosen to be there. A single piece of handmade ceramics with a story, a simple sculpture with personal meaning, a beloved book casually left on the table – these carefully selected details speak much more to the soul than an entire collection of forgotten objects accumulated without criteria.

The living room's aroma also composes its invisible personality. An electric or reed diffuser with essential oil of lavender (for calm), geranium (for emotional balance), or sweet orange (for joy). Good quality incense burned occasionally (like sandalwood or frankincense for elevation). Aromatic candles with soft, natural scents. All these elements create olfactory trails remaining in the affective memory associated with home. The living room's scent is often the first sensory impression upon entering. And it should be soft, pleasant, but present. Something silently communicating: "here is safe, here it's good to be, relax."

Soft music playing low in the background, the delicate sound of wind chimes from the balcony or window, or even the murmur of water from a small tabletop fountain – all these auditory resources can be used to create a living room that also listens, cradles, breathes in sonic harmony with its inhabitants.

Furniture should be, above all, functional and comfortable, but can also carry symbolic dimension. A well-organized bookshelf isn't just storage; it shows what intellectually nourishes residents, their interests, passions. A small side table with an open diary, a still-warm teacup, a lit candle – this isn't just random decoration, it's a small visual narrative about the habits and rituals of those living there. The living room should tell the story of its residents, but tell it lightly, organized, with pauses and breaths. Like a good book, where each chapter has its place and importance, but there's white space between lines for the reader to breathe, reflect, absorb content.

And, finally, but not least importantly, there's the invisible presence accumulated in the space. What isn't directly seen, but deeply felt. Conversations held there, silences shared with complicity, emotions overflowing – joys, sorrows, fears, hopes. All form an energetic layer, a subtle atmosphere impregnating the environment. Caring for the living room also means caring for this subtle memory. Performing regular energetic purifications with intention (using smoke, sound, salt, visualization). Opening windows daily, allowing sun and fresh air to touch all corners. Renewing furniture arrangement periodically, reordering objects, perceiving when something no longer vibrates with current energy and replacing it with something new, true, necessary for the present moment.

The living room, when harmonized and continuously cared for, becomes the living, pulsating heart of the home. It pulses. And each beat of this pulsation is a silent celebration of presence, of the life happening there. A space to receive others generously, but also to receive oneself, welcome oneself in moments of solitude or introspection. Fertile territory where harmonious coexistence, restorative rest, the simple joy of being together, belonging, is cultivated. May your living room tell the world who you are, authentically and beautifully. May it welcome your moments of sharing and your necessary creative silences. May each corner of it be a permanent invitation to encounter – with others and, fundamentally, with yourself. Because in the harmony of physical space, life's harmony blossoms. And everything begins, and always renews, in the heart of the house.

Chapter 24
Nourishing Kitchen

A sacred fire resides in the heart of the house. Its nature transcends mere symbolism; it physically warms, transforms matter, nourishes the body, and connects souls. This primordial fire dwells in the kitchen, that vital space where nature's elements – earth, water, fire, air, metal – mix in constant alchemy, where evocative aromas rise into the air awakening memories and appetites, where the invisible of intention merges with the tangible of ingredients in the fundamental gesture of feeding. The kitchen is, in its energetic essence, the womb of the home. It is the place where raw matter converts into vital sustenance, where daily alchemy transforms simple ingredients into complex affective memories, family traditions, health. When consciousness permeates this space, it ceases to be a simple functional room, a place for domestic chores, and becomes a true temple of nutrition, a radiating center of abundance, care, and manifest love.

Cooking, when performed with presence and intention, is an act of profound love – for oneself and others. But this love begins to be sown long before the pot goes on the fire. It starts with a careful look at the very space where the magic happens. In existential Feng

Shui, the kitchen is seen as the vital center of the house, intimately linked to residents' health, prosperity, vitality. Its impeccable organization, constant cleanliness, general energetic harmony have a direct, significant impact on the energy of everyone sharing that home. A neglected or chaotic kitchen can subtly undermine health and hinder the flow of abundance. A cared for, vibrant kitchen, conversely, nourishes on all levels.

The marked presence of the fire element, so essential and characteristic in this room, should never be neglected. The stove is its undisputed focal point. Much more than a simple appliance, it symbolically represents the power to transform – both raw foods into nutritious meals and, metaphorically, the very reality of those living there, through the energy of action and manifestation. A stove kept clean, well-cared-for, with all burners and oven functioning perfectly, is an active, powerful symbol of prosperity, capacity to generate sustenance and vital warmth. Neglect at this specific point is not just a practical issue of hygiene or functionality; it reverberates energetically as a sign of scarcity, carelessness towards one's own source of nutrition, stagnation in the ability to transform and create. Keeping the stove clean and functional is, symbolically, keeping the house's sacred fire alive and honored.

Each flame lit on the stove, each pot heated on it, each food prepared there carries an intention, even if unconscious. This is why the cook's state of mind, thoughts, feelings during meal preparation also directly influence the final result, not just in taste, but in the food's energetic quality. The kitchen demands mindfulness, presence. It naturally rejects automatism, stress, haste, careless impulse. Feeding is an act of creation, energy donation. Food, by its receptive nature, absorbs the energy of the preparation moment. A simple soup made in silence, calmly and lovingly, can heal more deeply than many words. A cake baked with genuine joy, intending to celebrate, warms the soul more than any blanket.

Furniture and object arrangement in the kitchen also deserves careful attention to ensure harmonious flow. Unobstructed, clean, organized countertops convey a sense of fluidity, facilitate movement, allow more conscious, pleasant food preparation. When space is free, movements tend to become slower, more careful, more respectful of ingredients and the act of cooking itself. Excessive accumulation – rarely used appliances on the counter, utensils hanging everywhere, forgotten jars in corners – creates visual noise, hinders cleaning, blocks smooth Chi circulation. The invitation here is to functional simplicity, valuing what is truly necessary, useful, and ideally, beautiful. Organizing cabinets and drawers, discarding what's no longer used, grouping similar items, optimizing space, greatly contributes to a sense of order and efficiency.

The refrigerator is another point of energetic power within the kitchen. Often neglected in its internal organization, it is the repository of vital energy to be ingested by the body. Expired foods, forgotten at the back of shelves, spoiled or poorly preserved items not only occupy precious physical space – they carry a vibration of stagnation, waste, "dead" energy. Keeping the refrigerator consistently clean, organized, with fresh, visible, easily accessible foods is like purifying the source from which vital energy will be distributed to residents. Using transparent containers, labeling leftovers, doing a weekly content review are practices helping keep this energy flowing healthily.

The same principle applies to the pantry or cabinets where dry foods are stored. Shelves crammed with packages and cans, packages opened months ago losing their properties, products piled without purpose or logical organization – all prevent food from being treated respectfully and abundance flow from circulating consciously. An organized pantry, with items grouped by type, airtight containers for grains and flours, clear visibility of what one has, functions as the house's nutrition map. It reveals eating habits, what's really consumed, what might be in excess, what's missing. It is also a symbolic expression of the house's collective unconscious. Someone accumulating food excessively, far beyond necessity, might be nurturing a silent fear of lack, insecurity about provision. Someone keeping everything hidden, disorganized, might be symbolically denying or hindering access to their own abundance and nourishment.

Colors present in the kitchen directly influence appetite, mood, willingness to cook and eat. Warm tones – like sunny yellows, vibrant oranges, stimulating reds (used moderately), welcoming earthy tones – evoke vitality, joy, energy, stimulate appetite. However, they shouldn't be used excessively, to avoid creating an agitated or heavy environment. Balance with neutral (white, light gray, beige) or light colors (pale blue, mint green) allows light to expand, space to breathe, a feeling of cleanliness and freshness. A wall painted a vivid color as a focal point, a patterned, colorful tablecloth or dish towels, a bowl of fresh fruit on the counter – these are small color points activating the kitchen's vibrational field without overwhelming senses, bringing joy and dynamism.

Aroma is another powerful ally in creating a nourishing kitchen. The unmistakable smell of freshly brewed coffee in the morning, fresh herbs being chopped on the board, garlic and onion gently sautéing in olive oil – all anticipate nourishment, prepare body and mind to receive food, even before it reaches the mouth. Aromas not only activate the palate but also awaken deep emotions, affective memories, feelings of comfort and belonging. Therefore, use aromas intentionally. A sprig of fresh rosemary in a glass of water on the sink corner brings protection and vitality. A small pot of mint or basil on the table or windowsill offers freshness and connection to earth. An infusion of spices like cinnamon and clove simmering gently on the stove on cold days brings comfort. Each natural scent has the power to reconnect to ancestry, childhood, nature's generosity.

Speaking of nature, one cannot overlook the importance of the living presence of fresh foods in the kitchen. Fresh, colorful fruits displayed in a beautiful fruit bowl on the table or counter, visible vegetables in airy baskets (if appropriate for their preservation), fresh herbs growing in small pots in the window. All this not only decorates but invites more conscious eating, more connected to natural cycles, more organic. Life generates life. And when this life becomes visible and accessible in the kitchen, there's a daily, powerful reminder that nourishing isn't just a mechanical act of ingesting calories – it's living in tune with the earth, seasons, food's vital energy.

The place where meals are eaten should also be honored and cared for. A table set with attention and care, even simply for everyday use, transforms the meal from a banal act into a small sacred ritual. Cloth napkins instead of paper, a lit candle in the center of the table (even during the day), a small centerpiece with flowers, leaves, or seasonal fruits. Eating with beauty, attention to detail, is a way of expressing gratitude for the food, everyone involved in its production, one's own body for its ability to receive and transform it into energy. Avoid eating hastily in front of the television, standing in the kitchen, or with the mind scattered by worries. These habits dilute nourishment energy, fragment presence, turn the sacred act of eating into mere automatism. Digestion, both physical and energetic, is harmed.

If there's a breakfast nook or dining space integrated into the kitchen, let it be an extension of this care and intention. No accumulating bills, mail, clothes to iron, or disconnected objects on the dining table. Food energy should circulate freely, without interference from other activities or concerns. External order facilitates internal digestion and appreciation of the present moment.

Words spoken during food preparation and meals also hold energetic weight influencing the quality of what's consumed. Constant complaints, heated arguments, judgments about food or others – all are energetically absorbed by the environment and, consequently, by the food. The kitchen environment, by its very alchemical, transformative nature (linked to the Fire element), functions as an energetic amplifier. Use this field wisely, consciously. Cooking while listening to soft, cheerful music, chanting a gratitude mantra, or simply in meditative silence allows food energy to be elevated, making it more nutritious on all levels.

It's also possible to create a small altar in the kitchen, a focal point of intention and gratitude. It doesn't need to be ostentatious or necessarily religious. It can be just a discreet corner on a shelf or counter, with a beautiful stone found in nature, a small plant, an image evoking gratitude for abundance (like an ear of corn, an image of Demeter or Lakshmi), or simply a candle. A place where, before starting food preparation, one can take a deep breath for a moment and offer a silent intention, like: "May this food nourish me on all levels – body, mind, and spirit" or "Gratitude for the abundance on my table." The kitchen, when treated thus, ritualized, truly transforms into a space of blessing.

When the kitchen is shared with other residents, it's fundamental everyone participates, somehow, in maintaining its harmony. Sharing cleaning and organization responsibilities, cleaning joyfully and cooperatively (instead of resentfully), preparing meals together whenever possible. These practices strengthen family or community bonds, dissolve tensions, transform daily chores into meaningful, nourishing moments of coexistence.

Always remember: it's not about seeking unattainable perfection or turning the kitchen into a decoration magazine scene. The nourishing kitchen is a real, living, dynamic, changeable space. There will be days with dishes piled in the sink, tiredness leading to improvised meals, reheated leftovers. And that's okay. What's important is that the base energy, the predominant intention, is of care, presence, respect for what happens there – the daily miracle of transforming matter into life. Because eating is one of the most intimate, fundamental, powerful acts that exist. It is, literally, incorporating the outside world. It is making what is outside an essential part of oneself. When this process is surrounded by consciousness and beauty, the kitchen becomes not just another room in the house, but a warm, vibrant heart, pulsing life, health, abundance energy throughout the home. And in this harmonious pulsing, the physical body strengthens. Interpersonal relationships warm up. The soul reconnects with the source of universal nourishment. The nourishing kitchen, then, is not just where one eats. It's where one learns, every day, to live with more awareness, more sensory pleasure, deeper gratitude. Where food is recognized as seed, fire, flower — all at once. Where the home reveals itself, perhaps more than in any other space, as the true center of healing and vitality.

Chapter 25
Tranquil Bedroom

The body incessantly seeks rest, a safe harbor where it can anchor after daily crossings. The mind yearns for silence, a space free from the turbulence of incessant thought, where quietude can finally settle. The soul, in turn, seeks retreat, an intimate refuge to process experiences, dream, and simply be. It is in the bedroom that these three essential dimensions of our being find, or at least should find, a shelter capable of welcoming, nourishing, and deeply regenerating them. This room transcends the mere functionality of being a place to sleep; it configures itself as the sacred space where we dissolve the layers of the external world, where the noises of daily existence finally cease, where eyes close not just to physical darkness, but so the vast inner universe can reveal itself in its fullness.

A truly tranquil bedroom does not represent a dispensable luxury, but rather a vital necessity. When the space dedicated to rest vibrates in harmony, the entire tapestry of life begins to pulse at a different rhythm, more serene, more connected, more alive. The bedroom functions as a personal sanctuary, an intimate, inviolable territory. Regardless of being a shared or solitary space, it is there that vulnerability finds permission to exist without masks, where the deepest dreams are gestated in the mists of the unconscious, where the accumulated fatigue of the day dissolves into long, liberating sighs. The wisdom of Feng Shui recognizes in this environment a central, irreplaceable role in maintaining physical, mental, energetic health. The energy we cultivate in this space reverberates through all other areas of our existence.

The bedroom deserves, therefore, care far exceeding simple aesthetic concern. It needs to be consciously built and maintained as a welcoming nest, a protective cocoon where the metamorphosis of rest can occur, an intimate temple where every element invites conscious disconnection from the external world and deep immersion into the inner universe.

The first concrete step to transform a common bedroom into a genuine space of serenity lies in understanding that rest is a complete, integrated sensory experience. It's not just about closing eyes and waiting for sleep to arrive. The body feels, vision absorbs, hearing registers, breath deepens or quickens, touch perceives, the overall sensation settles in. Absolutely everything composing the environment – colors painting walls and dressing the bed, textures caressing skin, sounds filling or disturbing silence, odors floating in the air, furniture arrangement guiding energy flow – directly influences the quality and depth of rest. Every detail communicates, even in dimness or total darkness. Every element is a note in the symphony of sleep. Attention to these details is, therefore, fundamental.

It begins with the bed, much more than simple furniture; it is the sacred altar of sleep, the stage where the unconscious enacts its dramas and revelations. Its position in the room is crucially important. Ideally, the headboard should be solidly against a firm wall, without gaps or instabilities, and never directly under windows, as this configuration transmits a sense of energetic security fundamental for deep relaxation. The solid wall behind the head functions as a protective shield, allowing the body to surrender to rest without the unconscious need for vigilance. It is also highly recommended that, from the lying position, one can see the bedroom entrance door, though not directly aligned with it. Facing the door directly can generate too direct, agitated energy flow, while being completely turned away creates vulnerability. Oblique view of the door offers a subtle sense of control, support, protection, calming the nervous system even unconsciously.

The bed's physical structure should be firm, stable, and above all, comfortable, proportional to the available space size. An excessively large bed in a small room can generate a claustrophobic feeling of oppression, hindering relaxation. An overly small bed in a very large room can, conversely, transmit insecurity or helplessness. Dimensional balance is key. The mattress, this intimate territory of deep rest, deserves special attention. It should be good quality, offering adequate support to spine and body. Its periodic replacement should be considered, not just for physical wear, but because it absorbs, night after night, not only body weight but also emotional loads, tensions, routine worries. It becomes an energetic record of our nights.

A point often neglected, but of great energetic impact, is the space under the bed. Categorically avoid storing objects there. Suitcases, boxes with old documents, accumulated shoes, out-of-season clothes: all create blockage in the flow of vital energy (Chi) that should circulate freely under the body during sleep. This upward flow nourishes and restores the energetic body. Emptiness under the bed allows Chi to circulate unimpeded, favoring truly deep, restorative rest. Accumulation, even invisible to eyes during the day, creates a persistent field of energetic stagnation projecting onto sleep quality, potentially leading to restless nights, disturbing dreams, or feeling tired upon waking.

Bedding acts as symbolic skins enveloping the body during sleep's most vulnerable state. Natural fabrics, like good quality cotton, linen, or silk, allow skin to breathe and create a tactile experience of pure coziness and comfort. Soft, tranquil colors – like pastel shades of blue, lavender, light green, beige, pale pink, or white – visually induce tranquility and relaxation. Avoid very vibrant patterns, excessively stimulating colors (like intense red or orange), or synthetic fabrics, which can generate excessive heat, skin irritation, interfere with the feeling of natural welcome. The bed should be a visual invitation to rest. Its image should evoke softness, comfort, peace.

Bedroom walls, likewise, should participate in this dialogue with silence and calm. Avoid very intense or dark colors, which can be oppressive or too stimulating for a resting environment. Paintings with disturbing images, excessive abstraction, or evoking conflict should be relocated to other house spaces. Excess visual objects on walls or shelves creates mental noise. The bedroom is, par excellence, the territory of visual calm. It's where eyes should find rest even before closing for sleep. One or two genuinely inspiring images, a personal symbol evoking peace and protection, a beloved object bringing positive affective memory – this is sufficient. Excess, once again, reveals itself as the sneaky enemy of deep rest.

The presence of electronic devices in the bedroom deserves special, redoubled attention. Television, though a common habit for many, directly interferes with sleep quality and environmental energy. Even when off, the device's physical presence continues emanating an electromagnetic field that can disturb the human energy field during sleep. It also functions as a symbolic portal to the outside world, full of stimuli, information, dispersion, exactly opposite of what's sought in a rest sanctuary. Ideally, television shouldn't be part of bedroom furniture. If removal is unfeasible, create rituals to minimize impact: cover it with a light, opaque cloth at night, unplug it (avoiding standby light), establish a usage time limit, turning it off at least an hour before sleep.

Cellphones, tablets, laptops follow the same logic. These devices should ideally sleep outside the bedroom, charging in another room. The temptation to check notifications or browse the internet before sleep or immediately upon waking is one of the biggest saboteurs of restorative rest. If keeping the phone in the room is necessary (as an alarm clock, for example), place it as far as possible from the bedside, preferably in airplane mode or completely off. Never use these devices in bed immediately before sleeping. Blue light emitted by screens drastically interferes with melatonin production, the natural sleep-regulating hormone, prolonging mental wakefulness even when the body already begs for pause.

Bedroom lighting should be designed to follow the sun's natural rhythm: brighter, clearer during the day, if possible using natural light, becoming progressively softer, warmer at dusk, culminating in near-total darkness at night. Fixtures with intensity control (dimmers), lamps with warm light bulbs (yellowish), candles (used safely), or amber-toned bulbs create an atmosphere signaling body and mind it's time to relax, slow down. Light functions as a subtle, powerful language. The body instinctively understands when it says: "now it's time for pause, retreat." Complete darkness at night is essential for restorative sleep. Blackout curtains are excellent allies for blocking external light from streetlights, car headlights, neighboring buildings. This light blockage allows the body's circadian cycle to regulate more precisely, optimizing melatonin production and entry into deeper, more restorative sleep phases. Sleeping in bright environments or with lights on, even dim ones, disrupts natural biological rhythm, negatively affects deep sleep quality, and can, long-term, interfere with immunity and other physiological processes. When absolute darkness isn't possible, sleeping masks made of soft, comfortable fabric can be great allies.

Sound also composes the invisible architecture of rest. Constant or intermittent external noises should be minimized as much as possible. Sealing window gaps, using thick sound-absorbing rugs, or rearranging furniture might help. When eliminating external noise isn't feasible (like in busy urban areas), using white noise (a constant, neutral sound masking others), recorded nature sounds (rain, ocean waves, gentle wind), or specific frequency music for relaxation (like binaural sounds or soft ambient music) can help create a soundscape more conducive to sleep. Absolute silence, when present and comfortable, should be celebrated. However, most important isn't total absence of sound, but creating an auditory environment that cradles and calms, rather than alerting or disturbing.

Adequate ventilation is another vital element for a healthy bedroom. An environment without air circulation becomes energetically thick, dense, stuffy – both physically, from carbon dioxide and humidity accumulation, and energetically, from Chi stagnation. Whenever possible, keep a window open part of the day for air renewal. In the morning, open curtains and windows for sun to enter and purify the space. At dusk, before sleep, allow a gentle breeze to circulate, clearing energetic remnants from the previous night and preparing the environment for a new rest cycle. Moving air is fundamental for keeping the bedroom's invisible field clean and vibrant.

Plant presence in the bedroom is welcome and beneficial, provided there's adequate ventilation for gas exchange at night. Species like lavender (whose scent is proven relaxing), jasmine, peace lily (helps filter air toxins), or the popular snake plant (known for purification, energetic protection) not only purify air but also bring nature's softness and vitality to the resting environment. Avoid, however, excess plants or species with very strong, stimulating scents. In the bedroom, the watchwords are delicacy and balance.

One shouldn't forget the floor greeting us upon waking. Soft, comfortable rugs placed beside the bed make a big difference in the transition from sleep to wakefulness. The first touch of feet leaving bed should be welcoming. A warm, pleasant surface symbolizes the day's initial contact with the physical world. May this touch be a gesture of care and comfort, not a shock of coldness or roughness.

At the bedside, simplicity should reign. Keep few, significant objects. An inspiring book, a stone with calming energy (like amethyst or rose quartz), an image evoking peace and serenity, a small diffuser with a soft, relaxing scent (lavender, chamomile, sandalwood are excellent options). Excess visual information or accumulated objects beside the bed fragments the sleep's vibrational field, can keep the mind agitated. Simplicity at this point is the safest path to tranquility.

Finally, consider symbols present in the room. The environment should contain elements supporting the deepest intentions of the sleeper's heart. A couple might choose an image representing union, balanced passion, companionship, mutual respect. Someone seeking a romantic relationship might opt for a symbol of welcome, openness to love, strengthening worthiness and self-love. A person living alone might wish to have representations of self-care, self-knowledge, inner peace nearby. Fundamentally, the bedroom space should mirror, symbolically and intentionally, what the soul wishes to nurture and attract into life.

A tranquil bedroom isn't a static, immutable scene. It transforms organically along with the resident. It needs revisiting, reorganizing, re-energizing whenever a significant internal change occurs, be it a new life phase, healing process, or perspective shift. The bedroom is the most intimate reflection of the being's internal state. Therefore, no magic formulas or universal rules exist. What exists is the need for sensitive listening, attentive presence, clear intention. When all these elements align, the bedroom transcends its physical function and transforms into a true energetic womb. A place one enters burdened by day's demands and leaves renewed by rest's alchemy. Where sleep isn't just physiological pause, but profound daily rebirth. Where dreams find safe space to communicate messages. Where the body confidently surrenders. Where spirit finds true repose. Where silence, finally, says everything. May each night spent in your bedroom be a conscious return to the essential. May you there truly leave the world outside and remember, in deepest quietude and darkness, the unextinguishable light always pulsing within you. Because, ultimately, the tranquil bedroom isn't just a well-arranged physical space. It is a cultivated, reflected state of soul.

Chapter 26
Invigorating Bathroom

Between the first revitalizing contact of water on skin in the morning and the last dive into the restorative silence of night, there exists in the house a unique transitional space that, when properly harmonized, transforms into a true portal of renewal. The bathroom, often neglected in its energetic importance or treated merely as a strictly functional room, is actually the epicenter where what no longer serves our being dissolves. It is in this intimate environment that the physical body cleanses itself of the day's impurities, but it's also where the spirit finds opportunity to renew itself, releasing accumulated loads and tensions. It represents the sacred space of energetic release, deep physical purification, and symbolic liberation from invisible weights. When understood and experienced from this broader perspective, the bathroom transcends its basic function and becomes a personal sanctuary of reconnection, a spa for the soul integrated into the home.

The ancient wisdom of Feng Shui recognizes the bathroom as a particularly delicate point in the house's energetic dynamics. It's where vital energy, Chi, tends to drain, dissipate. Literally, through drains, flushes, pipes, and the constant water flow itself, the energy that should nourish the home can be inadvertently drained away. For this fundamental reason, all care given to this room is not just a matter of hygiene or aesthetics – it configures a crucial energetic strategy for maintaining the overall well-being of the residence and its inhabitants. A neglected, dirty, disorganized bathroom or one with plumbing problems functions as an energy drain, subtly depleting Chi from the entire house, which can manifest as fatigue, lack of prosperity, or a feeling of stagnation in residents' lives. Conversely, a bathroom treated with reverence, kept clean, organized, vibrant, transforms this natural outflow into a powerful current of spiritual, emotional, vital cleansing, benefiting the entire home system.

    The first concrete gesture of respect and care for this space is keeping it impeccably clean. And this cleaning goes beyond superficial appearance; it needs to be deep and conscious. Tiles should shine, reflecting light and purity. The toilet, the primary symbol of disposal, must always be spotless and with the lid down when not in use, minimizing energy loss. Mirrors, portals to self-image, must be spotless, reflecting clearly. The shower stall should be free of mold, soap residue, or accumulations denoting stagnation. Cleaning the bathroom should not be seen as just any routine task, but as a periodic purification ritual. With each cleaning, not only is physical dirt eliminated, but dense energies accumulated there are also consciously removed: negative thoughts, energetic remnants the bath carried away, emotional weights symbolically drained with the water.

Water, the central, defining element of this room, is the protagonist. It runs, washes, purifies, carries away what's no longer needed. But it also has the power to renew, revitalize, bring life. Therefore, its flow must be carefully tended. Constantly dripping faucets, leaking showers, jammed or hard-to-operate valves: all symbolically represent invisible losses, continuous wear, waste of vital energy and resources. A leaking bathroom suggests, symbolically, that something precious is being drained from residents' lives without awareness – it could be time, money, creative energy, physical or emotional vitality. Promptly fixing these leak points is much more than simple plumbing maintenance – it's a symbolic act of repairing one's own capacity to retain and nurture abundance in its various forms.

The arrangement of elements and organization within the bathroom also speak volumes about the place's energy. An invigorating bathroom values order and visual clarity. Hygiene products and cosmetics should not be cluttered disorderly on the sink or piled in shower corners. Visual clutter transmits mental and energetic confusion, and each unused bottle remaining there occupying space retains stagnant energy. The philosophy here is clear: less is more. Keep only what's essential, beautiful to your eyes, genuinely necessary for your care rituals. What doesn't fit these criteria should follow another path – be discarded, donated, relocated. Cabinets and drawers should mirror this same organization. Opening a drawer to find expired items, old broken hairbrushes, dried-up cosmetics, dingy or torn towels – all carry not just visual disorder, but an impoverished vibration of neglect. The bathroom functions as a direct mirror of our self-care, self-esteem. What we keep there, even hidden from others' view, intimately reveals how we see our own value and worthiness. Making physical space, eliminating the useless, reorganizing remaining items with beauty and functionality is like declaring, without words: "I care for myself, I value myself, I matter to myself and deserve a space reflecting my essence and well-being."

Lighting plays, once again, an essential role in creating an invigorating atmosphere. Whenever possible, natural light should be invited in. A bathroom with a window is a true energetic gift. Sun has natural cleansing, purifying properties; it elevates the environment's vibration. Even if just for a few minutes a day, allow sun rays to touch the floor, tiles, objects. Let air circulate freely, residual shower humidity dissipate, outside life enter and renew the space. When natural light isn't possible, artificial lighting must be chosen carefully. Let it be bright enough for functionality, but also soft, welcoming. Avoid excessively white, cold, harsh lights, reminiscent of clinical, impersonal settings. Warmer lighting (yellowish), well-positioned, perhaps with indirect light points or a dimmer to adjust intensity, can completely transform the room, converting it into a relaxation haven.

Colors used in the bathroom also play a relevant role in its vibration. Light tones, like white, beige, light blue, or seafoam green, tend to visually expand space, convey cleanliness and freshness. They are safe, effective choices for this room. However, a touch of color can be very welcome to warm and personalize the space, avoiding monotony. A bath towel in a vibrant earthy tone, a plant with intense green leaves, a decorative dark-wax scented candle, a small colorful painting. The balance between a light base and welcoming color points makes the bathroom cease being merely functional and perceived as a nook of comfort and aesthetic beauty.

Mirrors are points of great strength and meaning in this room. They expand physical space, double available light, reflect our own image, influencing self-perception. Therefore, they must always be impeccably clean, well-maintained. A dirty, stained, fogged mirror blurs not only the reflected image but also the place's energetic vibration. Avoid broken, chipped, poorly positioned mirrors (e.g., cutting off the head or directly reflecting the toilet). Let the mirror be an ally in building self-esteem, showing the best of who looks. Let it function as a frame for conscious presence, not a portrait of neglect or fragmentation.

Plants can – and should – be part of bathroom decor and energy, provided light and humidity conditions suit the chosen species. Some plants thrive particularly well in humid environments with little direct light, common characteristics of many bathrooms. Ferns, pothos, snake plants, peace lilies, some bamboo varieties are great options. They bring nature's living energy to the room, help purify air (absorbing certain toxins), elevate the space's vibrational frequency. A well-positioned, healthy, thriving plant has the power to instantly invigorate the room. It's like bringing a breath of forest, a fragment of wild nature, into the intimate space of transition and purification. Where green pulsates, there is vitality.

Small gestures and details can completely transform the energy and experience of being in the bathroom. Lighting an aromatic candle during a bath creates a spa-like, relaxing atmosphere. Using a beautiful, organized basket for used clothes avoids a sense of disorder. Placing a polished natural stone or crystal (like rose quartz or amethyst) on the bathtub edge or sink adds a touch of earth energy. Hanging a painting with a serene nature image (waterfall, forest, sea) can serve as a relaxing focal point. Using a soft, absorbent mat underfoot when exiting the bath provides immediate comfort. Each element, when chosen and positioned with clear intention, transforms the banal, routine into a true self-care ritual.

Aroma is also an integral, fundamental part of this sensory experience. Avoid synthetic, aggressive air fresheners, which only mask odors and can harm respiratory health. Prefer natural scent sources: pure essential oils diffused in small amounts, room sprays made with hydrosols and essential oils, handmade soaps with soft scents, sachets with dried herbs. Scents like lavender (relaxing), eucalyptus (refreshing, purifying), lemongrass (invigorating), rosemary (energizing) are particularly suitable for the bathroom. The bathroom's scent should suggest cleanliness, renewal, freshness, purity. A discreet diffuser, a handful of dried herbs in a small bowl, a scented sachet hanging discreetly behind the door – these are small details effectively changing the atmosphere and perception of space.

And then we arrive at the peak moment of the daily ritual: the bath. Whether shower or immersion, this is the culmination of purification and renewal. The body surrenders to the water element. The mind has the opportunity to release tensions. Water runs, touches skin, carries away physical and energetic impurities. It's crucial this moment is lived with presence, intention. Avoid hurried, mechanical baths, body on autopilot, mind wandering through worries or plans. Even if time is short, let the act of bathing be whole, conscious. When wetting your face, perceive water's texture, temperature. When soaping arms, feel your own touch, skin contact. When rinsing, visualize or intend that everything weighing down, no longer serving, also goes away with the water draining down the drain. It's not magical thinking, but directing energy and consciousness. Water cleanses. The body responds to this intention. Energy renews.

Herb baths can further enhance this process. Preparing a concentrated infusion with herbs like chamomile (calming), basil (energizing, protective), lavender (relaxing), rosemary (invigorating, mind-clearing), or coarse salt (for deep cleansing) and pouring this water from neck down after a conventional bath is an ancient, powerful practice. Each herb possesses its specific strength, energetic property. Each bath can have its clear intention: calm the mind, energize the body, cleanse the auric field. It can be a gift offered from self to self, an act of profound caring, energetic attention.

If there's a bathtub, let it not be just a decorative or underused object. Let it be used, even sporadically, as a temple of immersion, deep relaxation. A warm bath with Epsom salts, flower petals, intuitively chosen essential oils. Time dedicated to silence, perhaps with the main light off and just a candle flame lit. The body floats in warm water, the mind dissolves worries, the heart slows its rhythm.

Upon exiting the bath, the care ritual continues and completes. Wrapping oneself in soft, clean, possibly lightly scented towels. Wearing a robe welcoming the still-damp body. Applying moisturizing cream or oil with slow, conscious movements. Looking at oneself in the mirror with tenderness, acceptance. All this nourishes not only the physical body but also the emotional and energetic body. The invigorating bathroom is one allowing the cycle of cleansing and renewal to close completely, satisfactorily. It's the space where one enters carrying the day's weight and leaves feeling light, clean, renewed. Where water not only washes the body but also awakens consciousness. Where silence can be deep, yet full of meanings, insights. Where intimacy with oneself isn't seen as fragility, but as a source of strength, self-knowledge. Where self-care transcends vanity and becomes an act of profound reverence for the life dwelling within us.

Caring for the bathroom is, in essence, caring for one's own sacred ritual of daily rebirth. It's remembering, every day, that we are beings made of layers, cycles, constant transformations. And that, by consciously removing what no longer serves us, we open precious space for all we can still become, flourish, manifest. May each bath be a return to the source. May each trip to the bathroom be an invitation to conscious pause, purification. May each cleaning performed there also be a deep internal purification. And may, in this small, often underestimated space of the house, the great, transformative power of renewing oneself be revealed – always, deeply, truly.

Chapter 27
Productive Office

There exists in the house a special territory where the mind finds wings to fly, where abstract ideas seek concrete form, where focus deepens and finds lodging to flourish. This place, though often improvised amidst the home's dynamic, functions as the neuralgic point of connection between the vast inner world of inspiration and the external world of manifest action. The office – whether a room exclusively dedicated to this function, a desk strategically positioned in a quiet corner of the living room, or a space creatively adapted beside a bright window – possesses an intrinsically sacred function: sustaining and nourishing the energy of creation, deep concentration, and authentic expression of our potential.

Within the perspective of existential Feng Shui, the office is understood as the territory of manifest purpose, the stage where vocation finds voice and action. It's where one works, studies, writes, plans, projects the desired future. It's the space where intellect finds the necessary structure to organize itself and where spirit finds a free channel for expression. For this fundamental reason, this environment's energy needs careful cultivation, protection, maintenance at high vibration.

A truly productive, inspiring office isn't defined by the quantity of visual stimuli, presence of latest generation equipment, or adherence to latest corporate decor trends. It is, first and foremost, a place where creative silence can breathe freely, where the mind finds clarity, where workflow happens naturally, pleasurably. Genuine productivity, born from connection with purpose, not external pressure, arises from purest balance. It's not about accelerated, frantic movement, nor inertia, procrastination. It's about fluidity. And this fluidity can only fully manifest when the physical environment is in perfect tune with the needs of the body, mind, soul of its user. The workspace needs to offer adequate ergonomic support for the physical body, but also, perhaps even more crucially, emotional and energetic support for mind and spirit. It needs to welcome logical, analytical thought, but also allow fertile emptiness, the space of "not knowing," necessary for the new, unexpected, truly creative to emerge.

Choosing the work desk's position within the room is the first point of strength to consider. It's one of the factors most impacting the feeling of safety, control over one's work. Whenever possible, the desk should be positioned allowing the seated person to see the entrance door, or at least for peripheral vision to perceive who enters. This is the "command position" in Feng Shui. It's not about vigilance or distrust, but energetic perception. Working with one's back to the door generates a constant, unconscious feeling of vulnerability, as if something could "attack from behind," keeping the nervous system in a subtle state of alert, hindering deep concentration. Conversely, when facing or sideways to the entrance, there's an inherent sense of clarity, presence, control, safety, allowing the mind to relax and focus on the task.

The seated person's back should ideally be protected by a solid surface. A firm wall, a well-anchored, organized bookshelf, or even a stable screen can fulfill this function. This physical protection symbolically conveys stability, support. Avoid positioning the work chair with its back directly towards large windows or passageways, as energy flow (Chi) becomes too unstable, dispersive in these configurations. A good chair backrest is more than physical support for the spine; it's a powerful symbol. It represents support for one's own decisions, the firm base upon which projects and ideas are built and sustained.

The work desk, in turn, should reflect desired mental clarity: clean, organized, but also alive, inspiring. Avoid excess objects on the surface. The essential usually suffices: the main computer or notebook, a special pen bringing pleasure to writing, perhaps a small plant bringing life, an item genuinely inspiring (a photo, stone, quote). When the work surface is cluttered with papers, books, pens, various objects, thought tends to scatter along with the gaze. Visual chaos inevitably translates into mental chaos. A free desk, with breathing room, functions like a blank canvas: it invites creation, idea organization. And creation, to flourish, needs physical and mental space. Use organizers, wellcompartmented drawers, labeled folders: everything should have its designated place. A productive office needn't be sterile or impersonal, but must be orderly. Everything where it should be. Precious time shouldn't be wasted searching for lost papers, tangled cables, essential books. Clarity in external organization induces and sustains internal clarity. And it's this clarity nurturing focus, presence, total dedication to work.

Lighting is another fundamental pillar for a healthy, productive work environment. Natural light is always the best option, being free, synchronizing our biological clock, improving mood. If possible, position the desk near a window so natural light falls laterally, avoiding direct screen glare or shadow over the writing area. Allow daylight to accompany your tasks' rhythm. Morning sun is particularly stimulating, awakening the mind, warming the body for activities' start. Even on cloudy days, the mere presence of an outside view brings a sense of spaciousness, connection benefiting the mind. When natural light is insufficient or at night, choose fixtures offering warm-toned (yellowish), soft, well-distributed light. Avoid harsh ceiling lights, white fluorescents, very intense direct light sources, which can cause visual, mental fatigue. Lighting should welcome the gaze, facilitate reading, concentration, without assaulting or tiring.

Colors chosen for the office should dialogue with the type of activity predominantly performed there and the user's personality. Light, neutral tones like white, beige, light gray favor serenity, visual spaciousness, thought continuity. Soft blues and greens are known to stimulate concentration, calm, mental balance, great for tasks requiring prolonged focus. A strategic touch of yellow or orange can activate creativity, optimism, communication. Earthy tones like brown or ochre bring feelings of stability, security, grounding, good for activities requiring planning, structure. Most importantly, however, is harmony in the chosen palette. Excessively loud colors, very strong contrasts, very agitated visual patterns can break internal rhythm, generate anxiety, drain mental energy.

Office walls function as blank canvases for inspiration. They can contain images evoking your professional purpose, phrases nurturing daily motivation, symbols representing past achievements or future goals. But again, nothing in excess. One or two well-chosen, significant elements suffice to sustain the desired vibrational field. A painting of a natural landscape calming the mind during breaks. A mandala helping organize gaze and thought. A photograph connecting you to your life mission or inspiring people. The wall should be a subtle, positive stimulus, not a source of constant distraction or visual pollution.

Ambient sound also exerts powerful influence on productivity, well-being. For many people, tasks, absolute silence is the most fertile ground for deep concentration, emergence of original ideas. For others, soft background music can help enter a state of flow, total immersion in activity. Music choice is crucial: instrumental soundtracks (classical, soft jazz, ambient, minimalist electronic), nature sounds (rain, ocean waves, forest), or even specific frequencies like binaural beats, can favor different mental states. Music with lyrics can be distracting for tasks requiring verbal focus. What's important is experimenting, discovering what works best for each individual, each type of creative work, using sound as a conscious tool to shape the mental environment, whether seeking silence or a melody inspiring, sustaining flow.

An often overlooked aspect, vital for fluid creativity, is accepting the process, including temporary disorder. An excessively rigid home, where any sign of "mess" is suppressed, can stifle experimentation. Creating often involves spreading materials, testing combinations, scribbling, making mistakes, redoing. A truly creative space welcomes this intermediate phase. This might mean having a stain-resistant work table, easy-to-clean surfaces, good storage for *in-progress* projects (not just finished things), or simply a permissive attitude towards controlled, temporary disorder. Allowing "creative mess" validates the process, not just the final result.

Equally important is valuing leisure, contemplation. Creativity doesn't respond well to constant pressure. Brightest ideas often emerge in relaxation moments, when the conscious mind rests, subconscious has space to work. Therefore, creating "do-nothing zones" in the house is paradoxically essential for creative productivity. A hammock on the balcony, a comfortable armchair facing the window, a bench in the garden, a quiet corner simply to sit and observe. These spaces invite pause, reverie, silent incubation from which most unexpected insights emerge.

Creativity is also a bodily experience. The body thinks, feels, expresses. A home encouraging fluid creativity offers space for movement. A room where furniture can be moved aside to dance, a corridor to walk while reflecting, a corner with a mirror to experiment with postures or expressions, a comfortable rug to stretch. Incorporating elements stimulating the body, like a Pilates ball, elastic bands, even simple percussion instruments, can release tensions, awaken new ways of thinking through movement. Similarly, the presence of varied natural materials – clay, wood, stones, different textured fabrics, handmade papers, natural paints – stimulates senses, connects the creative process to a more tactile, organic experience. Touching, smelling, feeling materials' weight, temperature can awaken associations, ideas purely abstract thought wouldn't reach.

Fundamentally, a creative home is one reflecting, reinforcing the resident's belief in their own ability to create. It's a judgment-free space, where experimentation is welcome, "error" seen as part of learning. Decorating with one's own creations (even simplest), having inspiring quotes visible, keeping idea journals or notebooks accessible, all function as constant reminders of inherent creative potential. The house becomes a mirror saying: "Here, you can be yourself. Here, your ideas have value. Here, you are a creator." When the external environment validates the internal creative voice, fluidity happens naturally. The house ceases being just a place to live and transforms into a soul's studio, an active partner in the journey of expression, discovery, realization. May each corner of your home be a silent invitation for your unique voice to manifest, transforming the everyday into a constantly evolving work of art.

Chapter 28
Sacred Space

There exists a singular point in the house, a corner whose measure transcends square footage. Its essence resides not in material luxury or the demand for absolute silence, nor is it bound to a specific belief, religion, or defined ritualistic practice. This point flourishes from pure intention, nourishes itself on attentive presence, and blossoms in the loving repetition of a fundamental gesture: the act of sitting within oneself, turning towards the inner core. The sacred space, when established within the home, converts into fertile ground where the spirit finds shelter to reveal itself, rest serenely, rediscover connection with that divine spark pulsating incessantly beyond the whirlwind of daily routines and external world demands. It becomes an intimate refuge, an oasis of tranquility amidst everyday hustle.

The quest for a sacred space reverberates as a deeply rooted ancestral need in the human soul. Since civilization's dawn, humans felt the impulse to demarcate territories of transcendence, erecting simple altars, forming stone circles under open skies, dedicating specific corners to prayer, contemplation, leaving symbolic marks on remote cave walls. All these manifestations shared a common purpose: marking, on the physical, tangible plane, the palpable presence of the invisible, the mystery permeating existence. Today, even immersed in a complex web of unavoidable commitments, bombarded by omnipresent technology, pressured by fabricated daily urgencies, this primordial call for inner connection hasn't extinguished; on the contrary, perhaps it's even more necessary. The home, when truly recognized, honored as a living, pulsating extension of our own being, cries out to house a point of reconnection, an epicenter of silence, introspection. The goal isn't creating an alienating escape from the world, but establishing a constant reminder of who we really are in the essential quietude sustaining all manifestation, a beacon so we don't get lost in superficial appearances, external demands.

Creating this personal sacred space begins with deliberately consecrating a territory within the house, dedicating it exclusively to deep, attentive listening. No fixed rules or universal formulas exist for its conception, only living principles that must resonate with each individual's truth. The most fundamental principle is this place be authentically yours, a reflection of your inner quest. It should be intentionally reserved for conscious pauses, moments dedicated to spirit-nourishing practices, simple rituals leading you back to your center of balance, serenity. It can manifest as a quiet living room corner, a carefully positioned rug in the bedroom, a balcony bathed in morning silence, or even a special nook in the garden, under a friendly tree's shade. Physical size is indeed irrelevant. This space's true dimension resides in the vibration it emanates, cultivated by your dedicated, intentional presence. It must be a place that, merely upon contemplation, evokes an immediate sense of serenity, an invitation to retreat. An environment where the body can instinctively slow its frantic rhythm, where time perception dilates, allowing immersion in the present, where the agitated mind finally finds a point of quietude, clarity.

The first practical step involves carefully choosing this location. Walk through your house with the sensitivity of someone seeking the ideal spot for a precious seed to germinate. Observe attentively where there's less foot traffic, where natural light touches the room with particular softness, where outside world noises arrive more filtered, almost like a distant murmur. Once a potential candidate is identified, sit there for a few precious minutes. Allow yourself to feel the space. Perceive sensations emerging in the body. Breathe deeply, consciously. Close your eyes for a moment, turning inward. If the body responds with relaxation, if the chest opens in expansive feeling, if thoughts begin silencing like gently falling leaves, then you've likely found your power spot, the ideal location to anchor your sacred space.

After choosing, this space needs energetic anchoring, symbolic delimitation. This is achieved through carefully introducing symbols resonating with your personal journey. A beautiful cloth spread on the floor, perhaps with patterns evoking tranquility or spiritual connection. A special cushion, comfortable, inviting, serving as seat for your practices. A candle, representing inner light, consciousness flame. An image inspiring or calming – could be a nature photograph, abstract artwork, sacred geometric symbol. A stone collected on a meaningful walk, a shell bringing sea memory, a fresh flower celebrating impermanence, present moment beauty. Every object selected to inhabit this space must carry deep meaning for you. Must be placed with full awareness, clear intention. These elements' function isn't merely decorative; they act as guardians of the subtle field cultivated, activated there, helping maintain elevated, focused energy.

No manual exists on which objects are "right" or "wrong." Choice is deeply personal, intuitive. Some feel strong connection with religious images representing their faith: a Buddha statue, crucifix, image of an orisha or Hindu deity. Others prefer connecting through nature symbols, feeling telluric force of a raw crystal, lightness of a randomly found feather, solidity of a river-polished stone. Still others opt for elements marking their personal trajectory: photograph of a beloved spiritual master or mentor, handwritten letter containing words of wisdom, object inherited from a loved one evoking protection, continuity. The common thread uniting all possible objects isn't their form or material value, but the profound meaning they carry for the individual. They don't function as magic amulets, but as constant reminders of our essential nature. They are symbolic anchors establishing a visible bridge between the everyday world and the dimension of mystery, sacredness, transcendence.

At this space's heart, a lit candle's presence during practice moments can be particularly powerful. The living flame is a universal archetype of inner light, the consciousness fire never completely extinguished, even in darkness moments. It's the same primordial fire pulsing at our heart's center, the divine spark animating us. Candlelight, when lit with intention during meditation, prayer, or simple contemplative silence, creates a vibrational field of respect, clarity, focused presence. It helps delimit the ritualistic space, concentrate energy, functioning as a soul's beacon.

The practice performed in this space is equally free, adaptable to each person's needs, inclinations. Doesn't need to be complex or lengthy. Could be silent meditation for just five minutes upon waking or before sleep. Could be reciting a prayer whispered fervently. Could involve intuitive writing in a dedicated notebook, letting thoughts, feelings, insights flow uncensored. Could be listening to soft, inspiring music, eyes closed, allowing melody to touch the being's innermost fibers. Could be chanting a mantra calming the mind, elevating the spirit. Or could simply be sitting comfortably, breathing consciously, cultivating gratitude for the present moment. The sacred space serves whatever, in that specific instant, reconnects you to your essential core, your deepest truth.

This space's vitality key lies in constancy, creating a regular rhythm of encounter. Establishing a habit, however brief, of visiting your sacred space daily or few times a week, strengthens its energy. The soul, metaphorically, gets used to this retreat place. Over time, it transforms into a magnetic field of peace, clarity. Each time you sit there, it's as if a subtle veil lifts, facilitating access to deeper consciousness states. Breath tends to change, becoming slower, deeper; shoulders relax, releasing accumulated tensions; the mind gradually quiets its incessant flow. Space begins "holding" your intentions' energy, prayers, release tears, deep gratitude moments. It becomes a silent, compassionate mirror of your inner journey, a living record of your spiritual growth.

Regular purification of this space is therefore essential to maintain its potency. This includes both physical and energetic cleaning. Sweep the floor attentively, clean symbolic objects with a light dry cloth, replace fresh flowers when wilted, if any. Open the window to ventilate, let sunlight touch elements, if possible. Use energetic cleansing methods resonating with you: gently pass smoke from herbs like sage, palo santo, rosemary; spray a mist of water with few drops of lavender or frankincense essential oil; sound a bell or Tibetan bowl to dissipate stagnant energies. The specific method matters less than the intention behind it: keeping the vibrational field renewed, light, clear, alive. A sacred space accumulating stagnant energy loses its catalyst power. It needs to breathe in unison with you.

Music can be a powerful ally in creating the desired atmosphere. Tibetan bowl sounds, known for harmonizing qualities; devotional chants from different spiritual traditions; nature sound recordings, like running water, birds singing, wind in trees; soft flute or string instrument melodies; music specifically composed for meditation or relaxation. Sound has the ability to elevate the environment's vibration, facilitate altered consciousness states. However, deep silence also holds invaluable worth. Learning to be comfortably silent, without needing to fill it, is one of the most potent practices the sacred space can offer. Sitting and just listening to the body's subtle sounds, breath rhythm, the murmur of thoughts gradually dissolving in quietude — this deeply nourishes the soul.

The sacred space also reveals itself as a powerful refuge in transition or difficult times. A particularly challenging workday. Unexpected news shaking internal structures. End of an important cycle, like a relationship or job. A difficult choice needing clarity, discernment. In these moments, retreating to your sacred space, breathing deeply, lighting a candle, perhaps writing about feelings or simply allowing oneself to be with the present emotion, can bring surprising clarity. The house, in this sense, transforms into a therapeutic ally. Instead of just physical shelter, it also shelters, contains the soul's pains, fears, charms, offering a safe continent for emotional processing.

For families or couples, sacred space beauty can be shared, creating a point of spiritual union. A small family altar where objects representing shared values, intentions are placed. A place where all can gather silently for few moments, say a prayer together, have deeper, meaningful conversations, away from daily distractions. Children, particularly, often enchant themselves with these spaces. They understand, intuitively, naturally, that there is a "heart corner," a special place. Perceive that there one doesn't shout, run disorderly, compete. There one listens attentively. Feels with the heart. Cares for each other, the space itself.

It's a common experience that, upon creating, cultivating this space, people express surprise: "I didn't know how much I needed this." We live in an era of overwhelming excesses – excess information, sensory stimuli, external, internal demands. The soul, to flourish fully, desperately needs spaces where it can simply be what it is in essence: vastness, silence, connection. Creating a sacred space at home is, therefore, an act of loving resistance against fragmentation, superficiality. It's declaring to the world, primarily oneself, that amidst incessant noise, contagious haste, exists an inviolable point of silence, an accessible center of peace. A point where everything can begin anew, with each breath.

With time, dedicated practice, energy cultivated in this space begins overflowing. It ceases being isolated point, subtly permeates the rest of the house. The kitchen might gain atmosphere of greater presence, gratitude. The bedroom might become more serene, conducive to restorative rest. The living room, more welcoming, inviting genuine connection. The sacred, by its expansive nature, isn't contained. It spreads like waves on water. Transforms. Positively contagions the entire environment. And, perhaps most profoundly, the internal sacred space begins flourishing more vigorously. External practice nourishes, reflects internal practice. You start carrying this state of silence, presence with you, even outside home. Amidst traffic jams, supermarket queues, difficult work conversations. The essential altar is now within you. Consciousness candle burns at chest center. Subtle sound of inner peace can be heard even amidst external noise. The house, then, fulfills its highest, noblest function: faithfully mirroring what is most essential, true, luminous in its inhabitant. May each home house its own sacred space, no matter how simple or elaborate. May it be true, authentic, vibrant with its caregiver's energy. May it receive your joy laughter, healing tears, hope prayers. May you there meet yourself, the Mystery permeating everything, the deep peace no external circumstance can truly steal. Because where a corner dedicated to presence exists, flourishes a safe path back home — the inner home, starting within us, reflected, like a faithful mirror, in every corner we choose to inhabit with soul.

Chapter 29
Living Garden

There comes a moment when the very structure of the house seems to yearn to transcend its physical limits, its masonry walls. A broader breath seeks to emerge, a latent desire to reconnect with the world's vital pulse vibrating incessantly outside. This essential pulse of nature, however, need not be a distant or inaccessible reality. It can flourish right there, in the space adjacent to the home: in the forgotten backyard, on the sunny balcony, the terrace overlooking the city, or even in the modest planter adorning the kitchen window. The garden, in its purest, most fundamental manifestation, represents the sacred point of contact where the house meets the Earth – and simultaneously, where the resident rediscovers and touches their own primordial nature, often dormant due to urban life.

A living garden's vitality isn't measured by its size or the complexity of its landscape design. It can be a vast terrain adorned with ancient trees and winding stone paths, or it can fit, gracefully and abundantly, into just three carefully cultivated pots on a compact apartment balcony. What truly defines a living garden is the vibration emanating from it, the vital energy moving dynamically, perceptibly there. It's the constant presence of life in its uninterrupted transformation cycle – the hesitant sprouting of a new leaf, vigorous growth towards light, ephemeral, colorful blooming of a flower, natural drying of leaves in autumn, resilient rebirth next spring. A garden pulsing with this natural dynamic becomes a sensitive, revealing mirror of the home's soul and its inhabitants.

Direct contact with natural elements, even through simple, daily gestures, triggers profound, scientifically measurable effects on our integral well-being. Research consistently demonstrates stress level reduction, beneficial regulation of the autonomic nervous system (decreasing "fight or flight" response), increased creative capacity and mental clarity, significant mood improvement, even immune system strengthening. Modern science begins empirically proving what ancestral wisdom intuitively recognized millennia ago: touching green, feeling earth, observing plant cycles, something deep within us returns to its original state of balance, belonging. A silent recognition emerges, an ancestral cellular memory whispering: we belong to Earth, are intrinsic part of it.

Creating a living garden begins with a conscious choice: deciding to allow nature to actively participate in daily life, opening the home's doors to its healing presence. This permission is, itself, a gesture of profound humility, an act of attentive listening to natural rhythms, confident surrender to the inherent wisdom of seasonal cycles. It implies recognizing that, even residing in a predominantly gray, artificial metropolis, potential space always exists for life to germinate – provided there's intention, willingness to nurture it.

For those with a backyard, the invitation to gardening presents itself more broadly, generously. However, even in these cases, external space is often relegated to neglect, becoming a debris deposit, accumulator of unused objects, simply an area of energetic abandonment. Reversing this situation doesn't necessarily require major infrastructure works or hefty financial investments. It primarily demands attentive presence, willingness to interact. The first concrete step is cleaning: removing what no longer serves, clearing debris, letting earth breathe again. Then comes careful observation: where does sunlight hit most intensely? Where do cool shadow areas form? Where does rainwater naturally drain? Nature itself already offers valuable clues about where it wishes to flourish most vigorously. One just needs to learn to perceive its subtle signs.

Choosing plants composing the garden is a process combining practical knowledge, sensitive intuition. Of course, it's fundamental to observe specific site conditions – region's climate, amount of direct/indirect sunlight, soil type, drainage. But beyond these technical factors, an inner call exists, an inexplicable attraction connecting us to certain species. Some feel magnetically drawn to succulents' resilience, geometric forms; others, to flowers' intoxicating perfume, vibrant colors; still others, by the desire to harvest fruits from trees they planted themselves. No "right" or "wrong" choice exists in this domain.

Vibrational affinities exist. Each plant, according to various traditions, carries a specific Chi type, a unique energetic signature. Some are known for mood-lifting properties, others for calming nerves, still others for offering energetic protection to the environment. When assembling your garden, allow yourself to listen with the body, feel plants' energy. Let yourself be guided not just by practical reason, but also intuitive feeling, choosing those resonating with your soul.

For those residing in apartments or houses without external areas, physical limitation might seem an obstacle, but never an insurmountable barrier to creating a living garden. Creativity offers charming solutions: a vertical garden installed on the balcony wall, transforming limited space into a verdant panel; pots of different sizes strategically placed in the kitchen window, bringing life, color to the room; small herb gardens grown in hanging planters or well-lit shelves; trailing plants descending gracefully from bookcases, softening angles, adding movement. Plant life is extraordinarily generous, adaptable. Just a handful of fertile soil, adequate light access, right amount of water, and it finds its way to grow. Just a little attentive, loving care, and it responds with beauty nourishing senses, soul.

Aromatic herbs are particularly suitable, rewarding for smaller spaces. Rosemary, basil, mint, thyme, oregano, sage, chives, parsley – the list is vast. Besides being extremely practical in the kitchen, delicately perfuming the room, these plants establish a direct, powerful link between cultivation, food. The act of harvesting your own fresh leaves to prepare a revitalizing tea or season daily food is an ancestral gesture of profound reconnection with earth cycles, our sustenance origin. It's a way of returning dignity, sacredness often forgotten in modern rush to the act of eating.

Flowers, with their exuberance, delicacy, also play crucial role in living garden composition. Colorful geraniums, fragrant lavenders, multi-toned carnations, shy violets. Each flower possesses unique color, characteristic perfume, particular blooming, wilting time. Flowers are like messengers of impermanence, ephemeral beauty. They teach us about living the present fully, beauty residing in complete surrender to the moment. A garden welcoming flowers is a garden singing silent melodies, celebrating life in its most vibrant, transient forms.

And we mustn't forget the essential element of foliage – ferns with delicate fronds, monsteras with imposing, cut leaves, pothos adapting, growing vigorously, marantas seeming to pray at dusk. Deep greens, varied textures inviting touch, organic shapes moving gently at the slightest breeze. Leaves constantly remind us of breath, vital exchange between inner, outer worlds. They symbolize everything in life operates in rhythm, pulsation, continuous flow of giving, receiving.

Integrating Feng Shui principles into garden planning, care can further deepen this energetic, symbolic connection. A large, solid stone, representing Earth element, harmoniously positioned beside a small pond or fountain, symbolizing Water element, creates powerful visual, energetic dialogue between stability, fluidity. A wind chime, made of natural materials like bamboo or metal, hung on the porch or garden entrance, activates Air element with soft, healing sounds, helping move stagnant Chi. A small statue of Buddha, a guardian animal like lion or turtle, or deity inspiring devotion, protection, can anchor these qualities in space, transforming it into safe refuge. Soft light from solar lanterns or candles protected in lamps invites nighttime contemplation, creating magical, introspective atmosphere. A simple bench positioned under a tree's shade naturally becomes an altar of rest, connection with nature. Each element, when chosen, placed with clear intention, transcends its physical function, transforms into potent symbol, charged with meaning.

    Caring for a garden is, in essence, spiritual practice disguised as daily task. Requires dedicated time, patience observing nature's slow rhythms, attentive listening to plants' silent needs. Requires, above all, humble acceptance there will be days a plant sickens inexplicably, leaves fall prematurely, pests emerge as unexpected challenges. Nature doesn't operate on linear logic of static perfection; it's dynamic, impermanent process. And the gardener, interacting with this process, learns welcoming impermanence more serenely. Learns restarting after loss. Learns trusting intrinsic rebirth strength. Learns offering love, care without guaranteed predictable results.

    The act of watering plants, whether morning or evening, constitutes one of the simplest yet most potent rituals connecting with the present moment. Feeling fresh water run through fingers, hearing soft sound of drops touching leaves, earth, perceiving characteristic smell of moist earth rising. Each gesture, performed mindfully, becomes silent prayer, humble "thank you" to life insisting on growing, despite all adversities.

For those who, for various reasons – constant travel, lack of adequate light, specific housing conditions – cannot have living plants at home, other creative, effective ways exist to bring garden energy indoors. Paintings with evocative nature images – serene landscapes, lush forests, winding rivers, flowery fields. Enlarged photographs capturing natural details' beauty. Dried flower arrangements, preserving plants' form, beauty even after life cycle ends. Tabletop water fountains reproducing relaxing sound of running water. Diffusers with natural scents reminiscent of forest, like pine, lemongrass, eucalyptus. All these elements can evoke, even symbolically, green's healing, revitalizing presence.

And finally, the inner garden exists. The one not depending on physical space, but born from attentive contemplation, presence cultivation. A quiet home corner where one can sit, observe cycle of plants one has, however small. A place where one can simply look at the sky through the window, witnessing clouds dance or stars shine. A space where one lights a candle, breathes deeply, turning towards inner silence. This garden is cultivated in the soul, through mindfulness practice, gratitude. And its energy, subtle yet powerful, overflows to the entire house, impregnating it with peace.

Maintaining a living garden, whether physical or internal, is fundamentally maintaining conscious relationship with our own essential nature. Nature, in its intrinsic wisdom, functions as mirror of what we are in depth. Plants don't judge us, don't demand immediate results, don't rush us in our process. They grow in their own time, following organic, perfect rhythm. And, observing them, we are gently invited to grow too, flourish without haste anxiety, release what no longer serves us – like dry leaves falling making space for new – reborn stronger, more resilient after each inner winter.

A living garden introduces vibrant energy into the home that no decorative object, however beautiful, can truly replace. It purifies air we breathe. Balances environmental humidity. Reduces temperature on hot days. Attracts beneficial presence of birds, butterflies, bees, creating micro-ecosystem of interdependence. Establishes visible, invisible bonds with external environment, reminding we aren't isolated. But, above all, it has power to profoundly transform house vibration, making it lighter, more loving, more genuinely habitable. Makes it, finally, a true home. May each house, however modest its physical structure, find, cultivate its green corner. May there sprout not only leaves, flowers, fruits, but also fertile silences, felt prayers, renewed hopes. May the garden transcend mere landscape condition to become faithful companion on life's journey. May it grow in tune with its caregiver's being growth: with light, shadow, attentive care, unwavering faith in life's strength. Because in the simple touch between human hand, generous earth, resides profound wisdom no word can fully contain – only the lived gesture knows its extent. And it's in this primordial gesture of cultivation, connection that home rediscovers its deepest, truest root.

Chapter 30
Health and Vitality

Our home is much more than a collection of walls and a roof over our heads; it functions as a second skin, a direct extension of our own physical and energetic body. What surrounds us externally, the atmosphere we breathe indoors, the objects we touch, the light bathing the rooms—all of it resonates deeply within us, influencing our health, mood, and vitality in ways we often don't consciously realize. A home that becomes unwell, accumulating clutter, dust, dampness, or stagnant energies, tends to mirror this condition in its inhabitants. It's not uncommon to feel persistent fatigue without an apparent medical cause, a lingering despondency, difficulty concentrating, poor sleep, constant irritability, or aches that wander through the body. These can be subtle signs that the environment itself is unbalanced, crying out for attention and care. Conversely, a space that has been intentionally harmonized, that breathes freely, stays clean, and where energy flows unimpeded, becomes a powerful source of nourishment, regeneration, and vigor. The home ceases to be a passive backdrop and transforms into an active ally in maintaining and promoting holistic health. It doesn't just accommodate a healthy body; it actively participates in its creation, shaping and supporting it through daily processes of healing and strengthening.

The path to transforming the home into fertile ground for health and vitality begins with a shift in perception, an awakening from indifference. We must abandon the limited view of the house as merely a functional space, a storage for objects, or a stage for routine. It's crucial to recognize it as a living organism, an interconnected system that responds, feels, and pulses in sync with its inhabitants. When we treat it with this reverence, acknowledging its sensitive nature, it reveals itself as a powerful partner in our journey toward physical, emotional, and energetic balance. Every conscious adjustment made, every bit of care given to a forgotten corner, every choice favoring flow and purity, returns as a gift of well-being.

Natural light emerges as one of the main protagonists in this process of environmental healing. Its influence goes far beyond simply brightening spaces. Sunlight is an essential nutrient for life, regulating our internal biological clock, the circadian rhythm, which governs vital functions like sleep, waking, hormone production, and even our mood. Adequate exposure to daylight stimulates Vitamin D synthesis, crucial for bone health and strengthening the immune system. Sunlit environments tend to lift spirits, combat lethargy, and increase overall energy. A home that generously welcomes sunlight, allowing it to dance through the rooms throughout the day, is a home that breathes vitality. And a home that breathes inevitably fosters healing, well-being, and mental clarity. Simple gestures like keeping windows unobstructed, using lightweight curtains that filter light without blocking it completely, or cleverly placing mirrors to reflect light into darker corners exponentially amplify the sun's therapeutic power within the home. Sunlight doesn't just illuminate; it purifies, energizes, and balances.

However, the attention to light doesn't end at sunset. Artificial lighting plays an equally crucial role in maintaining health, especially at night. Modern culture has flooded us with bright, cool-white lights, often intense, which, while efficient for certain tasks, can be extremely detrimental to our natural biological rhythm. These stimulating lights, rich in the blue spectrum, signal to the brain that it's still daytime, suppressing the production of melatonin (the sleep-inducing hormone) and prolonging mental and physical wakefulness. This results in difficulty falling asleep, fragmented sleep, and a feeling of tiredness upon waking. Conversely, warm-toned lights—yellowish, amber, soft—mimic the light of dusk and the ancestral hearth fire, signaling the body to slow down, relax, and prepare for rest. Strategically using lamps with low-intensity bulbs, dimmer switches to regulate brightness, candles (used safely), or warm-colored LED strips creates a cozy atmosphere that invites rest and respects the natural physiology of sleep. When the home modulates its light according to the day's cycle, it becomes an extension of the body's wisdom, and the body, feeling understood and supported by its environment, responds with greater balance and vitality.

The quality of the air we breathe indoors is another fundamental pillar of health, though often underestimated. We spend a large portion of our lives in closed environments, and the air circulating within these spaces can be laden with invisible pollutants. Volatile organic compounds (VOCs) released from paints, varnishes, new furniture, cleaning products; formaldehyde present in plywood and some fabrics; dust mites, fungi (mold), bacteria proliferating in damp, poorly ventilated areas; pet dander; accumulated dust. All contribute to an indoor atmosphere that can trigger or worsen respiratory problems, allergies, headaches, fatigue, and difficulty concentrating. The cure, once again, starts with the basics: ventilation. Opening windows daily, even for a few minutes during winter, is essential to renew oxygen and disperse accumulated pollutants. Creating cross-ventilation by opening windows on opposite sides of the house enhances this renewal. Paying special attention to moisture-prone areas like bathrooms and kitchens, ensuring they have good exhaust or natural ventilation, is crucial to prevent mold growth, a known health trigger. Besides mechanical ventilation, nature offers its own purifiers. Plants like Snake Plant (which releases oxygen at night), Pothos, Spider Plant, Peace Lily, and Aloe Vera are known for their ability to filter certain airborne toxins. Their presence not only beautifies but actively contributes to a healthier environment. Using air purifiers with HEPA filters can be considered for severe allergies or high outdoor pollution. Avoiding harsh chemical cleaners and opting for natural solutions (vinegar, baking soda, essential oils) also reduces the toxic load in the environment. Breathing clean air at home is fundamental to keeping the body and mind vibrant.

Sound, or its absence, also plays a significant role in our health and vitality. We are immersed in constant cacophony: the hum of electronics, traffic noise, incessant phone notifications, the television droning in the background. This continuous noise pollution, even if we get used to it, keeps the nervous system in a subtle state of alert, raising cortisol levels (the stress hormone), increasing blood pressure, and hindering deep relaxation. A home that promotes health also cultivates silence or, at least, a harmonious soundscape. Identifying and minimizing sources of unnecessary noise is the first step. Unplug appliances when not in use, repair noisy ones, use headphones for individual activities. To muffle external noise, strategically using sound-absorbing materials like thick curtains, plush rugs, bookshelves, and upholstered furniture can make a big difference. In some cases, investing in soundproof windows might be a more definitive solution. Introducing healing sounds is also a powerful way to balance the home's sonic energy. Soft instrumental music, nature sounds (running water, birdsong, gentle rain), mantras, or specific frequencies (like Solfeggio or binaural beats) can create an atmosphere of calm and focus. Small indoor water fountains or pleasant-sounding wind chimes (placed where the breeze is gentle) add a touch of serenity. The key is to choose ambient sound intentionally, transforming it into a tool for well-being, a melody that soothes the nerves and uplifts the spirit, rather than an additional source of stress.

The tactile dimension, the experience of touch, connects us directly to feelings of safety and comfort, influencing our emotional state and, consequently, our health. A home filled with cold, smooth, hard, or synthetic surfaces can generate a subliminal sense of distance, a lack of coziness. The body craves contact with the natural, the soft, the warm. Incorporating materials like natural wood (in furniture, flooring, or objects), organic fabrics (cotton, linen, wool) in throws, pillows, curtains, and bedding, natural fiber rugs (sisal, jute, wool), and elements like stone or handmade ceramics creates a sensory richness that nourishes the nervous system. The simple act of walking barefoot on a wooden floor or a soft rug can have an immediate grounding effect. Wrapping oneself in a wool blanket on a cold day, feeling the uneven texture of a clay pot, resting hands on a solid wood table—these are micro-doses of comfort that communicate to the body: "You are safe, you can relax." A home that cares for health is also a home that caresses its inhabitants through textures, turning the environment into a sensory nest.

Order and cleanliness transcend mere aesthetics; they are pillars of vitality. A chronically disorganized environment, cluttered with objects, dusty surfaces, visible broken items, or crammed corners, creates a constant mental burden. The human brain seeks patterns and order, and visual chaos requires continuous cognitive effort to process or ignore, draining energy that could be used for other functions. Physical clutter often mirrors or induces mental and emotional clutter. Conversely, a clean, organized space, where everything has its place and the flow is unimpeded, promotes mental clarity, calmness, and a sense of control over one's environment. The regular practice of cleaning and organizing, when done with presence and intention, becomes a meditative act, a way of bringing order not only to the house but also to thoughts and feelings. Releasing what no longer serves (decluttering) opens up physical and energetic space for the new, for vitality to circulate. The energy saved by not having to deal with chaos translates directly into more energy and well-being.

The kitchen, as the nourishing heart of the home, exerts a direct and powerful influence on health. It's not just where we prepare our meals, but where the energy of food is transformed and from where the vitality that sustains our body emanates. A clean, well-lit, organized kitchen with easy access to fresh, healthy foods acts as an invitation to more conscious eating habits. The state of the stove, refrigerator, and pantry are direct reflections of our relationship with nutrition and, by extension, with self-care. A clean and functional stove symbolizes the ability to transform and nourish; an organized refrigerator with vibrant foods represents available vitality; a pantry free from excess and expired items shows awareness and respect for the flow of abundance. The act of cooking, when performed with calmness, presence, and positive intention, infuses the food with healing energy. The environment where meals are consumed also matters. Eating in a pleasant space, at a table, without distractions like screens, chewing slowly and appreciating the flavors, improves digestion and nutrient absorption, transforming eating into a ritual of health and pleasure. The harmonized kitchen nourishes body and soul.

Spaces dedicated to movement are equally essential for vitality, even in small homes. The human body was made to move, and physical stagnation often leads to energetic and mental stagnation. Creating a small corner that invites stretching, yoga practice, dancing, or any form of physical exercise is fundamental. It could simply be a mat unrolled in the living room, free space in the bedroom, or an adapted balcony. Having this space available and inviting makes it easier to incorporate movement into the daily routine. A body that moves is a body that breathes better, circulates energy, releases tension, and stays younger and more energetic.

Restorative rest, facilitated by a peaceful and harmonized bedroom, is perhaps one of the most critical pillars of health. As explored earlier, a dark, quiet environment with a pleasant temperature, free from electromagnetic pollution, and with elements that invite relaxation (soft colors, natural textures, calming scents) is essential for the body to carry out its nightly processes of cellular repair, memory consolidation, hormonal regulation, and detoxification. Quality sleep is the foundation upon which the next day's vitality is built. Neglecting the bedroom environment means neglecting one's own capacity for regeneration.

Beyond the physical aspects, the spiritual and emotional dimensions of the home are intrinsically linked to health. Having a sacred space, a small altar, or a corner dedicated to meditation, prayer, or simply quietude, strengthens the connection to life purpose, inner peace, and emotional resilience. Health transcends the physical body; it encompasses mental, emotional, and spiritual well-being. A home that nurtures the spirit offers a safe haven to process emotions, find clarity, and recharge subtle energies. Feeling emotionally connected to the home, feeling that it represents, welcomes, and supports you, creates a virtuous cycle of well-being. The house becomes a positive mirror, reflecting and reinforcing feelings of belonging, love, and security.

Health and vitality, therefore, are not the results of a single isolated factor, but rather a complex symphony where the environment plays a crucial role. The home, when cared for with awareness and intention, transforms into a silent conductor, orchestrating the rhythms of light and shadow, air and sound quality, the comfort of touch, the purity of nutrition, the invitation to movement and rest, and the embrace of emotions and spirit. It becomes a field of active regeneration, a personal sanctuary where the body can heal, the mind can balance, and the soul can flourish. May your home be this sacred territory of strength and well-being, a constant reflection of the vitality pulsing within you, and unwavering support on your journey to a full and healthy life.

Chapter 31
Fluid Creativity

The house we inhabit is not just a stage for our lives; it actively participates in the choreography of our thoughts, feelings, and, fundamentally, our ability to create. It thinks with us, whispers ideas in quiet corners, reflects our clarity or confusion on the surfaces surrounding us. A house that breathes, that has open spaces and circulating energy, becomes a powerful ally of the mind, a true incubator where imagination can germinate, ideas can take shape, and creativity can flow without obstruction. Far from being a gift reserved for artists or inventors, creativity is a vital impulse inherent in all of us, manifesting in how we solve daily problems, express ourselves in the world, reinvent our routines, and add color and flavor to existence. Cultivating a home that nurtures this fluid creativity is investing in our own capacity for adaptation, innovation, and authentic expression. The physical space, when harmonized with this intention, ceases to be a mere container and becomes a catalyst for the creative potential latent in every being.

Creativity, in essence, craves freedom. It doesn't flourish in cramped environments, overloaded with visual information, or energetically stagnant. It needs air to breathe, space to move, silence to be heard. Therefore, the primary ingredient of a home that stimulates creativity is, paradoxically, free space. This isn't about extreme minimalism or empty rooms, but rather the absence of barriers that confine the gaze and the mind. A room where the view can wander without stumbling over excess, a work desk with clear surfaces inviting materials to be spread out, a blank wall offering itself as a canvas for an inspiration board, a chalkboard for sketching fleeting ideas, a clear floor where one can sit to reflect. Open physical space mirrors and encourages the mental openness necessary for thought to explore new territories, for intuition to manifest without being stifled by clutter. Creativity needs this fertile emptiness to fill it with the new.

The second crucial element is appropriate stimulation, which is radically different from information overload. Creativity isn't born from sensory bombardment, but from subtle enchantment, aroused curiosity, the silent question an object or image might evoke. It involves a careful curation of elements that inspire without distracting. An intriguing design object on a shelf, a pillow with an unexpected texture inviting touch, an art or poetry book left strategically open, a musical instrument leaning against the wall like a silent invitation to melody, a box with colored pencils and various papers, a loom with work in progress, an unfinished piece of pottery. These are visual and tactile sparks that ignite the imagination, suggesting possibilities, inviting interaction, reminding us that the creative process is made of experimentation and discovery. These stimulation points can have a fixed place, like a studio or reading nook, but they can also be dynamic, migrating through the house according to need or momentary inspiration. A mood board updated with projects or seasons, a clothesline with ideas hanging, a collection of stones or shells telling travel stories, a vision board where dreams and goals are visualized—all keep creative energy moving, nourishing the mind with new perspectives.

Lighting, that invisible sculptor of atmospheres, plays a vital role in modulating the creative state. Natural light, with its rich spectrum and variation throughout the day, is unparalleled. It tends to stimulate lighter, expansive, optimistic thinking. Working or creating near a window, having a reading space bathed in afternoon sun, turning a sunny balcony into a small studio—all connect the internal rhythm to nature's rhythm, fostering clarity and inspiration. Sunlight, especially in the morning, seems to awaken the mind to new possibilities. When natural light is scarce, artificial lighting needs to be thoughtfully considered. Warm, soft lights are generally more conducive to prolonged creative work and introspection, while slightly brighter lights can be useful for tasks requiring detail or brainstorming sessions demanding more energy. The ideal is to have options: functional general lighting, adjustable desk lamps, floor lamps with amber light to create a more intimate and collected atmosphere at night. The ability to adjust light allows the environment to accompany the different phases of the creative process, offering the right luminous support for each moment, whether it be expansion, focus, or reflection.

Colors, with their distinct vibrational frequencies, dialogue directly with our brain and emotions, influencing the disposition to create. There's no single formula, as the response to colors is also personal, but some associations are frequently observed. Yellow is associated with mental clarity, optimism, idea generation. Orange can bring enthusiasm and energy to start projects. Blue, in lighter shades, favors imagination, expansive thinking, and communication, while deeper tones invite introspection and intuition. Green, the color of nature, promotes balance, calm, and growth, excellent for environments seeking sustained concentration. Red, the color of passion and action, should be used moderately, perhaps in details, to provide an energy boost or break monotony, but in excess can generate agitation. Violet or purple are linked to intuition, spirituality, and transformation, potentially inspiring for more artistic or introspective work. The key is to feel which color or combination resonates with the type of creativity one wishes to nurture in each space, using them on walls, furniture, objects, or artwork to create a visually stimulating yet balanced environment.

The home's soundscape also modulates creative capacity. For some people and tasks, absolute silence is the most fertile ground for deep concentration and the emergence of original ideas. For others, a soft musical background can help enter a state of flow, that state of total immersion in the activity. The choice of music is crucial: instrumental soundtracks (classical, soft jazz, ambient, minimal electronic), nature sounds (rain, ocean waves, forest), or even specific frequencies like binaural beats, can favor different mental states. Music with lyrics can be distracting for tasks requiring verbal focus. The important thing is to experiment and discover what works best for each individual and each type of creative work, using sound as a conscious tool to shape the mental environment, whether seeking silence or a melody that inspires and sustains flow.

An often overlooked aspect, yet vital for fluid creativity, is the acceptance of the process, which includes temporary disorder. An overly rigid home, where any sign of "mess" is suppressed, can stifle experimentation. The act of creating often involves spreading out materials, testing combinations, sketching, making mistakes, redoing. A truly creative space embraces this intermediate phase. This might mean having a stain-resistant work surface, easy-to-clean surfaces, good storage for projects *in progress* (not just finished things), or simply a permissive attitude towards controlled, temporary clutter. Allowing for "creative mess" validates the process, not just the final result.

Equally important is valuing idleness and contemplation. Creativity doesn't respond well to constant pressure. The brightest ideas often emerge during moments of relaxation, when the conscious mind rests and the subconscious has space to work. Therefore, creating "do-nothing zones" in the house is paradoxically essential for creative productivity. A hammock on the balcony, a comfortable armchair facing the window, a bench in the garden, a quiet corner to simply sit and observe. These spaces invite pause, daydreaming, the silent incubation from which the most unexpected insights emerge.

Creativity is also a bodily experience. The body thinks, feels, and expresses. A home that encourages fluid creativity offers space for movement. A room where furniture can be moved aside to dance, a hallway where one can walk while reflecting, a corner with a mirror to experiment with postures or expressions, a comfortable rug to stretch on. Incorporating elements that stimulate the body, like a Pilates ball, resistance bands, or even simple percussion instruments, can release tension and awaken new ways of thinking through movement. Similarly, the presence of varied natural materials—clay, wood, stones, fabrics of different textures, handmade papers, natural paints—stimulates the senses and connects the creative process to a more tactile and organic experience. Touching, smelling, feeling the weight and temperature of materials can spark associations and ideas that purely abstract thought might not reach.

Fundamentally, a creative home is one that reflects and reinforces the inhabitant's belief in their own ability to create. It's a judgment-free space where experimentation is welcome and "mistakes" are seen as part of learning. Decorating with one's own creations (even the simplest), having inspiring quotes in view, keeping journals or idea notebooks accessible—all serve as constant reminders of inherent creative potential. The house becomes a mirror saying: "Here, you can be yourself. Here, your ideas have value. Here, you are a creator." When the external environment validates the internal creative voice, fluidity happens naturally. The home ceases to be just a place to live and transforms into a soul's workshop, an active partner in the journey of expression, discovery, and fulfillment. May every corner of your home be a silent invitation for your unique voice to manifest, turning everyday life into a constantly evolving work of art.

Chapter 32
Emotional Balance

There is a deep resonance, a silent and continuous conversation between the space we inhabit and the universe we carry within us. Home and heart function as interconnected mirrors; the state of one inevitably reflects in the other. What pulses in our innermost being—our joys, fears, anxieties, and hopes—finds an echo in the home's atmosphere, while the environment's vibration, in turn, reverberates in every cell of our emotional body, influencing our mood, resilience, and ability to navigate life's tides. Emotional balance, that constant quest for a stable center amidst life's fluctuations, doesn't solely depend on internal practices like meditation, therapy, or self-knowledge. It is profoundly influenced and can be actively cultivated by the environment surrounding us. The home, when consciously harmonized, transcends its function as shelter to become a true emotional sanctuary, an invisible balm that supports, regulates, and sustains us.

A home vibrating in balance doesn't eliminate life's difficulties, but it offers a safe container to process them. It functions like the calm, steady presence of a wise friend, who doesn't need to offer solutions, but whose mere existence conveys safety and serenity. On sunny days, it celebrates with us; on stormy days, it offers refuge and perspective. It whispers to anxiety's ear: "It's okay, you are protected here." This fundamental sense of security, provided by a harmonious environment, allows the nervous system to relax, emotions to flow without becoming dammed up, and recovery after stressful moments to be quicker and more effective. The house becomes an external regulator helping modulate our internal states.

The first step in transforming the home into this emotional sanctuary is developing sensitive listening, not just to the physical space, but primarily to how we feel within it. One must become an attentive observer of one's own emotional reactions in different rooms or situations at home. Is there a corner that consistently evokes irritation or discomfort? Is there a place where breath seems to catch, or conversely, where one sighs with relief? Which areas are neglected, avoided for no apparent reason? What emotions predominate in the living room versus the bedroom? This emotional mapping of the home is crucial. It reveals how our energy field interacts with the environment's energy field, showing where blockages, tensions, or, conversely, points of strength and harmony exist. By bringing awareness to this dynamic, we can begin making intentional adjustments that promote greater balance.

Light, as we've seen, is a powerful tool for modulating atmosphere and, consequently, emotions. Chronically dark or poorly lit spaces can intensify feelings of sadness, apathy, fear, or insecurity. Constant dimness can weigh on the spirit. On the other hand, overly bright, white, artificial light can generate agitation, anxiety, and difficulty relaxing. Balance lies in the ability to adjust light to the needs of the moment and the function of the space. Natural light, whenever available, brings vitality and optimism. At night, transitioning to softer, warmer, indirect lighting signals the body and mind to slow down, promoting calm and introspection. Using dimmers, lamps with low-wattage bulbs, candles, or amber-toned lights can create islands of serenity that invite emotional relaxation. Light, used with intention, becomes a non-verbal language communicating safety and welcome.

The colors surrounding us act like notes in an emotional melody. Each hue carries a specific vibration that can uplift, calm, energize, or even disturb us. Earth tones (browns, beiges, ochres) promote a sense of stability, security, and connection to the earth, great for creating a calm base. Blues, especially lighter, softer shades, are known for their calming effect on the mind and nervous system, ideal for bedrooms or meditation spaces. Greens, reminiscent of nature, bring balance, freshness, and a sense of renewal, working well in living or work areas. Pale pinks and pastel tones evoke softness, tenderness, and compassion, usable for creating more welcoming and affectionate environments. Yellows and oranges, in balanced shades, can bring joy, optimism, and sociability, but in excess can be overly stimulating. White, though neutral, can bring clarity and purity or coldness, depending on how it's combined with textures and other elements. The conscious choice of colors, whether on walls, furniture, or details, allows tuning the environment's vibration to support the desired emotional state.

Scents, with their direct connection to the limbic system—the brain's emotional center—are incredibly effective tools for influencing mood and well-being. Certain smells can instantly calm anxiety (like lavender or chamomile), lift spirits (citrus like orange or bergamot), promote focus (rosemary or peppermint), or induce deep relaxation (sandalwood or ylang-ylang). Using essential oils in diffusers, natural room sprays, good quality scented candles, or even the natural aroma of fresh flowers, herbs, or cooking food can transform a room's atmosphere, creating an olfactory environment that actively supports emotional balance. Avoiding synthetic and aggressive odors, which can overload the nervous system, is equally important. The home's scent becomes a subtle signature of care and well-being.

Similarly, the home's soundscape profoundly impacts our emotional state. Constant, sharp, or unpredictable noises generate stress and tension. The sound of the TV on as background noise, frequent arguments, jarring alarms—all contribute to sensory overload that hinders maintaining inner calm. Cultivating silence, when possible, is a balm. When not, choosing sounds that promote harmony—soft classical music, nature sounds, mantras, healing frequencies—can help neutralize sonic stress and create a more peaceful environment. The quality of the sound surrounding us is a determining factor for emotional tranquility.

Order and physical organization of space have a direct correlation with the feeling of internal order. Chaotic, disorganized environments, cluttered with objects or dirt, tend to generate a sense of mental and emotional overload. The brain interprets external disorder as a subtle threat, a pending task, keeping the nervous system in a low-level state of alert. This hinders relaxation and the feeling of peace. Keeping the house reasonably organized, with simple systems for storing objects, clear surfaces, and a basic cleaning routine, frees the mind from this invisible burden. External clarity facilitates internal clarity, allowing emotions to flow more balancedly.

However, emotional balance doesn't mean living in a sterile environment or denying life's complexity. A home that supports emotional well-being is also one that welcomes vulnerability. There must be spaces where it's safe to feel and express the full range of human emotions—sadness, anger, fear, joy. A comfortable sofa where one can cry without judgment, a bed offering refuge on difficult days, a window where one can watch the rain and feel melancholy. The home shouldn't be a stage for perfection, but a nest offering unconditional safety to be who we are, with our lights and shadows. Accepting imperfection in the environment reflects and allows acceptance of our own humanity.

The images, artwork, and symbols we choose to decorate our home act as emotional anchors. Photographs of happy moments, landscapes evoking serenity, inspiring quotes, objects representing strength or resilience—all can reinforce positive emotional states and serve as visual reminders of our values and aspirations. It's equally important to be mindful of objects or images that might be charged with negative energies or associated with painful memories. Removing from the environment what no longer resonates with our present well-being is an act of emotional self-care, freeing the space (and ourselves) from past burdens.

Tactile comfort, provided by natural materials and pleasant textures, is another powerful language of emotional embrace. The sense of safety and well-being experienced when wrapped in a soft blanket, feeling the warmth of wood underhand, or stepping on a plush rug, activates the parasympathetic nervous system, responsible for relaxation and stress recovery. The house, through touch, can offer a constant hug, an invisible lap that comforts and stabilizes us.

Connection with nature, even indoors, is a proven emotional restorative. Plants, flowers, the presence of water (in fountains or aquariums), stones, wood—all these elements reconnect us with the slower, resilient rhythms of the natural world, helping regulate our own emotions. Caring for a plant can be a therapeutic act in itself, teaching patience, cycles, and the beauty of impermanence.

Incorporating small daily or weekly rituals in the domestic space also helps anchor emotional balance. Lighting a candle upon arriving home, sipping tea silently in a favorite corner, writing a few lines of gratitude before sleep, dedicating a few minutes to meditation in the sacred space—these acts repeated with intention create landmarks of stability and presence amidst life's fluidity, helping center the mind and calm the heart.

Finally, the emotionally balanced home is one that acknowledges and supports difficult times. It doesn't promise constant happiness but offers a safe refuge, solid ground where we can process pain, loss, or confusion. It becomes a silent therapist, a loving container allowing us to weather internal storms knowing we have a safe harbor to return to. The house we cultivate with consciousness and presence thus becomes much more than a physical address; it transforms into a mirror of our soul and a powerful instrument for balance, healing, and emotional flourishing.

Chapter 33
Lasting Harmony

The journey of transforming the home, when undertaken with consciousness and heart, rarely returns us to the starting point. Just as a long walk through unknown landscapes changes the traveler, the process of redesigning the space we inhabit—with intention, sensitivity, and presence—transforms us profoundly. By the end of this exploration, the home is no longer the same set of walls and objects; it has become a clearer mirror of our current essence, a living expression of the present, and a vibrant platform for the future we wish to build. The harmony achieved, however, is not a trophy to be stored on a dusty shelf. Lasting harmony is a dance, a state of dynamic and continuous flow between the being who inhabits and the space that welcomes, a silent dialogue that adapts and evolves to the rhythm of life's cycles.

Achieving and, more importantly, sustaining this harmony is like developing a new level of intimacy with one's own home. The initial phase, perhaps marked by a more conscious effort to reorganize, clean, declutter, and decorate with purpose, gradually gives way to a loving naturalness in caretaking. It becomes less about "applying techniques" and more about "being in relationship." It's like the gardener who, after preparing the soil and planting the seeds, continues to observe, water, prune, and nourish the flourishing garden, knowing it needs constant attention to remain vibrant. It's like parents watching their children grow, adapting care to new phases, offering affection, establishing flexible routines, and maintaining attentive listening to their changing needs. The house, as a living organism, is not static; it changes because we change. And the harmony permeating it, to be lasting, needs to be equally fluid and adaptable.

The master key to this enduring harmony lies in the practice of continuous listening. Harmonizing the home is not a one-time event with an endpoint. It's a cyclical process. The house pulses in resonance with the inhabitant's internal tides: changes in mood, health, relationships, priorities, life stages. Each of these subtle or significant alterations calls for adjustments in the environment so it continues to serve as adequate support. Keeping the habit of "conversing" with the house alive is essential. This might translate into periodically walking through the rooms with a fresh eye, sitting in different corners just to feel the energy, noticing if areas have begun accumulating clutter or seeming stagnant, questioning if a space's function still matches current needs, or simply noting if something cries out for change, renewal, release.

This review can be anchored in nature's rhythms, becoming a seasonal ritual. Each change of season offers a natural invitation to realign the home. Spring, with its expansive energy (Wood element in Feng Shui), might be the ideal time for deep cleaning, bringing in more plants and vibrant colors, opening windows to let fresh air circulate. Summer, with the predominance of the Fire element, invites simplifying environments, favoring ventilation, creating outdoor living spaces. Autumn, ruled by Metal, is conducive to introspection and letting go—a great period to organize closets, donate what's no longer needed, prepare the house for greater retreat. Winter, associated with Water, calls for coziness, warmth, introspection—time to add blankets, rugs, soft lighting, create reading nooks and rest areas. Aligning home care with nature's cycles (and, by extension, our own internal cycles) helps maintain harmony organically and intuitively.

In shared homes, lasting harmony intrinsically depends on mutual participation and respect. It cannot be imposed by a single person; it needs to be co-created. This requires open dialogue about how everyone feels in the space, what their needs are, and how the environment can support everyone's well-being. Defining shared responsibility zones, establishing agreements on organization and cleaning, creating respected personal spaces, and perhaps holding "house meetings" focused not on problems but on how to improve the feeling of home for everyone, are strategies that strengthen bonds and collective harmony. Caring for the space becomes an act of caring for the relationships flourishing there.

Incorporating small maintenance rituals also helps anchor harmonious energy in daily life. It could be something simple like dedicating 15 minutes daily to tidying up before bed, choosing a day of the week for more conscious cleaning (including energetic aspects like lighting incense or playing soft music), or having a monthly moment to reorganize a specific closet or drawer. These rituals transform home care from a heavy obligation into a mindful practice, a constant gesture of affection that prevents clutter and stagnation from settling in again.

Lasting harmony also flourishes when there's openness to the new and to change. A house that remains unchanged for years, despite its inhabitants' internal transformations, eventually becomes an obsolete setting, an energetic brake. Allowing the home to evolve with us is fundamental. This doesn't mean rampant consumerism or constant renovations, but rather the flexibility to make small changes reflecting who we are *now*. Moving a piece of furniture can completely alter a room's dynamic. Introducing a new color in pillows or on a wall can bring renewed energy. Replacing an old photograph with a more recent one, or an object that lost meaning with something inspiring in the present moment, are gestures that keep the house alive and aligned with the personal journey. The space should be a stage for the present and an invitation to the future, not a museum of the past.

Sustainability, in this context, reveals itself as a natural partner of long-term harmony. Making conscious choices—opting for durable, responsibly sourced materials, preferring second-hand or restored furniture, repairing objects instead of immediately discarding them, reducing overall consumption, using eco-friendly cleaning products—not only benefits the planet but also the home's energy. Less waste means less stagnant energy associated with trash and disposal. Conscious choices carry a positive intention that permeates the environment. A home respecting Earth's resources tends to have a more balanced, stable, and coherent vibration.

Regular energetic cleansing, as explored earlier, is another essential pillar for maintaining the home's vibrational clarity over time. Whether through smudging with herbs, using sound (bells, bowls, mantras), sprays with essential oils, candlelight with intention, or simply opening windows to sun and wind, it's important to purify the environment periodically. This removes accumulated energetic residues from stress, conflicts, illness, or simply the intensity of daily life, ensuring Chi can flow freely and the atmosphere remains light and revitalizing.

And, perhaps the most powerful ingredient of all for lasting harmony, is the constant practice of gratitude. Being thankful for shelter, comfort, beauty, the safety the home provides. Thanking each corner that welcomes us, each object that serves us, each meal that nourishes us. This gratitude, expressed silently or aloud, elevates the space's vibration incomparably. It transforms the relationship with the house from one of possession to partnership, from an acquired right to a received blessing. Gratitude is the invisible cement binding all elements and sustaining the home's energetic structure.

When inhabiting a house where harmony has become a continuous state, the feeling transcends mere beauty or organization. One perceives a deep settling, a sense of "being home" permeating every cell. Time seems to flow more kindly. There's space to be, feel, create, love, rest. Tension finds no place in corners, stagnant energy doesn't hide behind doors. There's pulsating life, circulating like air, water, light. And this vitality is sustained by attentive presence, constant care, loving dialogue between inhabitant and space. The house, finally, reveals itself not as a passive setting, but as a living entity that collaborates, responds, and heals. May your home continue to be this luminous mirror of your evolving essence, a garden flourishing with you, supporting your path with beauty, simplicity, and a deep harmony that, once discovered, reverberates throughout your life.

Epilogue

Some journeys don't require a passport. Nor distance. Not even luggage. They ask only for silence, listening, and presence. And upon reaching the end of this reading, perhaps you realize you've already embarked on one of those journeys—not outward, but inward. This wasn't just a book about houses. It was a crossing about belonging, awareness, and rebirth.

Something subtle has changed. Maybe you can't name it yet. Perhaps it's a sweet discomfort looking at the sofa where you sit every day. Or a feeling of tenderness passing by the entrance, now aware that it welcomes—or pushes away—everything that arrives. Perhaps an unexpected urge to open windows, move furniture, empty drawers. Or maybe something deeper: the quiet certainty that your house can, indeed, become a healing reflection of your soul.

This book didn't bring promises. It brought possibilities. And the most precious among them was recovering the lost link between environment and essence. Between form and function. Between the invisible and the tangible. With each chapter, we discovered there's no neutral object, mute wall, or harmless space. Everything vibrates. Everything communicates. Everything shapes—and is shaped by—us.

Understanding home as a living organism is more than a metaphor: it's a reunion with the sacred lost in excess, haste, the mechanization of dwelling. Rediscovering the value of natural light, the presence of plants, the breath of materials, the fluidity of Chi... is remembering that the external world begins within. And that the space we occupy is not just our setting—it's our mirror, our temple, our oracle.

Perhaps the most profound transformation proposed by this work is precisely this: exchanging automatism for intention. Replacing "letting be" with "caring for." Transforming routine into ritual. And thus, inhabiting the house as one inhabits one's own story—with listening, reverence, love.

If you've come this far, something inside you has already moved. Has already shed old structures. Has already begun, even discreetly, to make peace with the space sheltering you. And that, in itself, is a revolution. Because transforming home is also assuming the role of author of one's own destiny. It's moving from being a tenant of chaos to becoming a gardener of energy. It's declaring: "Within here, life flourishes."

And the beauty of this transformation is that it doesn't demand perfection. It doesn't require an ideal style, a generous budget, an Instagrammable environment. On the contrary: it's born from welcomed imperfection, soulful improvisation, the simple gesture carrying intention. A consciously lit candle illuminates more than an exuberant chandelier. A pot with a single plant, cared for with presence, vibrates more than a shelf full of soulless objects.

True Feng Shui—as revealed in these pages—doesn't impose formulas. It invites listening. It reminds us that life pulses with rhythms that cannot be forced, and that each house has its own personality, history, silences. Wisdom lies in dancing with it, conversing with it, allowing it to reveal what needs to be seen.

And more: this book planted the seed of a broader ethic. An ethic of care. Because whoever learns to care for their own space naturally extends that care to others, the neighborhood, the city, the planet. By reconnecting with nature's cycles within the home, the desire to protect Earth's cycles is also born. This is how the small gesture—opening a window, removing excess, placing a flower—becomes part of a great movement.

May this book not end here. May it reverberate in every reorganized corner, in every revitalized environment, in every new breath your home inspires. May you continue observing with renewed eyes, listening with more sensitivity, creating spaces that sustain your best version. Because the house, now you know, is not where one resides. It's where one lives. And living with presence is the greatest luxury there is.

The journey through the healing house doesn't end with the last page. It merely begins. With each new choice, each conscious gesture, each morning you wake up and feel that space welcomes you—there, once again, healing happens.

Continue. The path is open. The space is alive. The soul is home.

www.ingramcontent.com/pod-product-compliance
Lightning Source LLC
LaVergne TN
LVHW040042080526
838202LV00045B/3447